Man and his Past

O. G. S. Crawford

Copyright © BiblioLife, LLC

This historical reproduction is part of a unique project that provides opportunities for readers, educators and researchers by bringing hard-to-find original publications back into print at reasonable prices. Because this and other works are culturally important, we have made them available as part of our commitment to protecting, preserving and promoting the world's literature. These books are in the "public domain" and were digitized and made available in cooperation with libraries, archives, and open source initiatives around the world dedicated to this important mission.

We believe that when we undertake the difficult task of re-creating these works as attractive, readable and affordable books, we further the goal of sharing these works with a global audience, and preserving a vanishing wealth of human knowledge.

Many historical books were originally published in small fonts, which can make them very difficult to read. Accordingly, in order to improve the reading experience of these books, we have created "enlarged print" versions of our books. Because of font size variation in the original books, some of these may not technically qualify as "large print" books, as that term is generally defined; however, we believe these versions provide an overall improved reading experience for many.

MAN AND HIS PAST

BY

O. G. S. CRAWFORD

HUMPHREY MILFORD
OXFORD UNIVERSITY PRESS
LONDON   EDINBURGH   GLASGOW   COPENHAGEN
NEW YORK   TORONTO   MELBOURNE   CAPE TOWN
BOMBAY   CALCUTTA   MADRAS   SHANGHAI   PEKING
1921

TO
JOHN LINTON MYRES
WYKEHAM PROFESSOR OF ANCIENT HISTORY, OXFORD

PREFACE

I DESIRE to express my acknowledgements to the following for permission to reproduce illustrations : to Mr. S. Hazzledine Warren for the photograph of the Palaeolithic Wooden Spear-head facing p. 16, to the President and Council of the Society of Antiquaries for the photographs of the Mortlake Bowl and Beaker facing pp. 19 and 80, to the Delegates of the Clarendon Press for plates facing p. 111, to Mr. J. Challenor Smith, F.S.A., of Silchester, for plate facing p. 164, to H.M. Stationery Office for the Sketch-map of the Ancient River Solent (reproduced from *Memoirs of the Geol. Survey*, Ringwood Sheet, 1902, p. 32) and for the map at the end of the book (reproduced from Ordnance Survey, Hants, Sheet 76, N.W.).

My most grateful thanks are due to Dr. Alfred Cox, O.B.E., for his kindness in undertaking to read the proofs.

O. G. S. CRAWFORD.

ABSTRACT OF CONTENTS

CHAPTER I

INTRODUCTORY 1

    The idea of the earliest (flint) implements as 'extra-corporeal limbs'—the growth of brain through development of the sense of touch, concomitantly with the growth of power of intelligent co-ordination of hand and eye to chip a flint—a premium thus, for the first time in evolution, set upon intelligent rather than automatic response.

    Incidentally there is put forward the suggestion that an important factor in man's evolution may have been a period of desiccation which ended a long forest régime, and compelled our arboreal ancestor to become at last wholly terrestrial. There his tactile proclivities had full scope in making ' eoliths ', a pastime which ultimately secured his survival, and *pari passu* developed his intellectual power. ' While he was chipping the blade of his stone axe, man was at the same time giving a keener edge to his own faculties.'

CHAPTER II

THE HISTORY OF MAN 24

    The value of a study of *tools* (the *disjecta membra* of man's extra-corporeal evolution) is thus evident ; and tools (the raw material of archaeology) logically include the aeroplane as well as the axe. What, then, is the distinction between archaeology, anthropology, and history ? Marett's description of anthropology as the whole study of man. This is often lost sight of by specialists in each department, who fail to realise the unity of the trinity. This unity is of the first importance, for it is the scientific counterpart of universal brotherhood (in ethics) and of the ' parliament of man ' (in politics). It broadens the specialist's outlook, and thereby raises all his work to a higher plane ; it removes the danger of provincialism from the study of local history, etc. ; and provides a justification of all ' human ' research however intricate or remote, because the raw material of education is thereby being accumulated.

CHAPTER III

WHAT IS ARCHAEOLOGY ? 38

Its subject-matter is sherds, flints and earthworks. These are no longer regarded as ' curios ' to be explained by historical narratives, but as touchstones to verify or condemn them ; and as documents from which to construct our account of pre-historic times. It is the method of Sherlock Holmes. Epigraphy is a special department of archaeology, but so special that it is usually best left to specialists. It is to archaeology what palaeography is to history, but less important, because for many regions and periods no inscriptions survive. A man may be a good archaeologist without being able to decipher inscriptions, just as a man may be a good lawyer without being able to engross. Archaeologists would do better to confine their probationary years to (for example) making themselves proficient in soil-study, surveying, photography, drawing, human anatomy and the preservation of antiquities, all of which are indispensable accomplishments

The archaeology of existing primitive peoples is an almost untouched field, but it must wait until we have studied the fast-vanishing cultures of the living. The opportunities will never recur, and buried sites can safely be left. At the moment we want an anthropologist, whose heart is rather in European prehistory, to make a complete, geographical study of a small primitive group. For he alone will direct attention to those points upon which *archaeologists* require most enlightenment.

All the methods of archaeology and anthropology are paralleled in the work of the intelligence department of an army in the field ; the identification of units from caps and badges, the interpretation of earthworks on air-photos, the ' historical evidence ' of prisoners, critically examined.

CHAPTER IV

ARCHAEOLOGY AND HISTORY 48

The aim of archaeology being to find out all possible about the men of past ages, what is its relation to history ? History as described by Myres (*The Value of Ancient History*, Oxford, 1910). Adopted, with a corollary on the value of the history of their own country to other peoples, *e.g.* of India, Egypt and the Sudan. This is a practical question for an imperial people.

ABSTRACT OF CONTENTS

But how to discover the 'history' of a people (like the Sudanese) without any historical documents? By archaeological excavation. History thus written, however, falls short of true history, for it fails to ' distinguish the fool from the sage '.

Archaeology can help history by confirming or contradicting its facts ; as, for example, is now being done in England with the Anglo-Saxon chronicle by Saxon archaeologists : and it can supplement it, especially by regional researches (concerned with castles, moated manors, homesteads, forest perambulations and the like). Archaeological material so used, however, is inferior in value to the material remains of prehistoric man, which remains are the only evidence we have. Hence the word ' antiquary ' might be reserved for the students of ' historic ' archaeology.

A paragraph to guard against a possible misunderstanding. By advocating the unifying of human history, I do not wish to propose any drastic reorganisation of the existing working arrangements (learned societies, etc.). That will come in time, but must come from within, and spring from a real desire, prompted by a change of spirit and widening of outlook. Such a change is urgently needed if we are to see the wood and not only the trees, as at present. A great deal of published research would be better unpublished, and the historical journals reserved for articles of a more general character.

CHAPTER V

ARCHAEOLOGY AND ANTHROPOLOGY . . . 56

Archaeology, like history, but with the reservations above mentioned, is a department of anthropology. A confusion of thought, however, arises from a double use of the word anthropology, sometimes to denote ' the whole study of man ', sometimes departments of it, such as the study of living primitive peoples, and human anatomy. It were better to invent a separate word for the whole study of man and call it ' andrology ' (but this word is reluctantly suggested and not pressed into use here except where unavoidable). ' Andrology ' has three main stages : (1) long prehistoric ; (2) short culminating historic ; (3) widely extended present.

Analysis of contents of some European anthropological journals, to discover proportion of archaeological articles. Discussion of how far the publication of archaeological and anthropological articles in the same volume is desirable.

The recognition of their position in the philosophic trinity would benefit the work of archaeologists, historians and anthropologists by widening their outlook. Only historians refuse to come into line. Their pre-eminence is undisputed, and would not suffer.

CHAPTER VI

THE METHODS OF ARCHAEOLOGY 65

Archaeological work founded on the evolution and classification of types (Evans' *Bronze Implements*). The value of *association* in formulating a chronological framework (bronze hoards). Stratification and the geological parallel. Type-fossils. The complicated basis of the chronological scheme of Britain, remote from Egypt the ultimate reference of all European chronology. The value of potsherds, and the art of distinguishing them.

CHAPTER VII

TIME-ASPECT AND SPACE-ASPECT 78

The isolation of periods, resulting from type-study, leads to an intensive study of regions and cultures. How to ascertain the geographical limits of a culture, illustrated by an example. Conclusion—archaeology is *a* time-aspect (the one which is concerned with man); geography is *the* space-aspect. Geology is the principal extra-human time-aspect. Time and space and their gradually narrowing relativity (the universe, the earth, Europe, England and ourselves). Some analogies from geology.

CHAPTER VIII

THE IMPORTANCE OF ENVIRONMENT . . . 89

' A study of its environment is essential to a proper study of any organism ; so, too, the study of the environment of a group of organisms ; and when we come to groups, the environment at once becomes geographical.' But before they can study groups, archaeologists have got to *reconstruct* the environment of vanished groups and cultures ; and this requires the co-operation of workers in other branches of science. Examples of the way in which prehistoric distributions can be explained by reconstructed biological environment. The need of an Atlas of Geographical Environment; its Mediterranean, Atlantic, and Pacific orientations.

ABSTRACT OF CONTENTS

CHAPTER IX

ARCHAEOLOGY AND OTHER BRANCHES OF SCIENCE .   PAGE 95

Geography as the space-aspect; Sir Charles Close's Presidential Address; the non-existence of anything that can be called 'pure' geography. Mineralogy and botany; how mineralogists can help us. Metals, amber, flint and their connection with trade-routes. Again a geological parallel: as the archaeologist traces trade-routes by the occurrence of exotic objects, so the geologist reconstructs ancient river-courses from the occurrence in gravel of rocks foreign to the locality, or glacial drift by erratic blocks.

CHAPTER X

THE MAIN FACTORS IN MAN'S ENVIRONMENT . . 107

General remarks on position, climate, soil, vegetation and other animals, and how to reconstruct maps of them.

CHAPTER XI

MAN'S INFLUENCE UPON HIS ENVIRONMENT . . 120

The turning of the tables upon nature. The gradual diffusion of the environmental control illustrated by the progress of invention; *e.g.* man was at first dependent upon the inhabitants of a few distant regions for his supply of tin, essential for making bronze; later, the discovery of iron opened out many new sources close at hand. 'The process is throughout a liberating process, because it destroys the binding monopoly of a single, or restricted, source of supply, or of the people of a peculiarly favoured district.' The discovery of agriculture, and the need of tracing the history and spread of cultivated plants—wheat, maize, olive, vine, fig, palm, orange. The importance of honey, before the sugar-cane and sugar-beet were known. The horse and its introduction into Europe.

The study of all these points is the business of naturalists, not archaeologists, hence the need of a broader and more anthropocentric basis of education to open the eyes of the coming generation of scientists.

CHAPTER XII

'Value' in Archaeology 128

    Archaeological specimens are of value to their owner precisely in proportion to the use he can make of them—or, as we say, to the 'value he sets upon them'. They may mean nothing to him, or everything. Isolated finds are often considered valueless to the ungeographical archaeologist, because he does not know how to extract anything of value from them. This can be done by marking the site of the discovery of *all* upon a map, and then seeing what conclusions can be drawn from their distribution. Pitt-Rivers on the exclusion of the word 'importance' from scientific dictionaries.

CHAPTER XIII

Distributions 132

    What we may expect to learn by studying the distribution of types, and what each class of object is capable of telling us, *e.g.* pottery shows habitation-areas and only rarely trade-relations (because pots break in transit and every one can make their own at home). Axes, gold ornaments and rare objects show trade, and also confirm the habitation-areas already revealed by pot-distribution. The interpretation of *chance* finds (*i.e.* objects which have been both lost and found again by accident) and how far they may be used to indicate trade-routes. The representative nature of a single find of a gold ornament; many more were never lost, or lost and not yet found, or refound only to be melted down. The value of taking the distribution of more than one object of a period as a check upon accidental disturbing factors, *e.g.* the presence of a big museum or energetic collector or excavator in the district. Sea-borne trade. The meaning of 'influence' in archaeology.

CHAPTER XIV

Old Roads and Lines of Communication . . 154

    Wessex as an enchanted castle of upland pastures, surrounded by the thorny hedge of lowland clay-forests. The passes into Wessex over watersheds or fords, or through gaps in the forest or sea-wall (harbours). The nuclear character of Salisbury Plain and within it again of Avebury and Stonehenge.

ABSTRACT OF CONTENTS

CHAPTER XV

PAGE

ROMAN ROADS: GENERAL METHODS AND ARCHAEOLOGICAL EVIDENCE 163

The necessity of specialisation in research, and the reasons for selecting Roman roads here as an example.
What they were made of (local material). General characteristics. How they were rediscovered in a number of selected instances, illustrating the value of preconceived ideas, if you are prepared to throw them overboard when necessary. Advice to the field-archaeologist.

CHAPTER XVI

ROMAN ROADS: DOCUMENTARY EVIDENCE . . 195

Peutinger Tables; Antonine Itineraries; Anglo-Saxon boundaries; mediaeval documents; old maps; the note-books of older field archaeologists (Leman). Parish boundaries. The author's survey of the Roman roads of Wessex; the desirability of similar surveys of other regions and the fascination of the work.

CHAPTER XVII

EXCAVATION 208

The need of experience under a master before beginning to dig: then the prime necessity is to make good plans. The number of men to employ, and the advantages of a small over a large gang. Trial trenches or surface-clearing. The value of a good navvy who knows his soils. The cleaning out of silted ditches and graves. Why objects found at the bottom of a ditch are valuable. Pitt-Rivers' experiment at Wor Barrow. The whole subject too big for complete treatment here.

CHAPTER XVIII

MUSEUMS 215

Reasons why museums at present repel rather than attract: partly due to their own dust and disorder; partly (because good museums are hardly more successful) to their divorce from education. A change can only come by reforming education and bringing it into line with the ideal museum. This change is coming, and is foreshadowed by the growing demand for Universal History. The ideal World Museum described; it will be in America, and will begin with a representation of the birth of the solar system, and proceed through the geological record, to the present and even the future, ending in a single room containing (as a warning and an incentive) a model of the moon. Such a museum will become in time the goal of holiday pilgrimage throughout the world.

CHAPTER XIX

Conclusion 225

The 'use' of archaeology is as difficult to describe as the 'use' of art. Archaeological research is pursued as an end in itself, but it is pregnant with value for humanity.

LIST OF ILLUSTRATIONS

Ancient Earthwork on Ham Hill, Wilts		*Frontispiece*
		PAGE
Palaeolithic Wooden Spear-head, found at Clacton, Essex	*Facing*	16
Neolithic Pottery Bowl, found in the Thames at Mortlake	,,	19
The Mortlake Beaker	,,	80
Sketch-map of the Basin of the ancient River Solent	.	105
View on Woodcott Down, Hants, showing lynchets and junipers	*Facing*	111
Natural vegetation on Litchfield Down, Hants	,,	111
Bronze Sword, found in the Thames, near Battersea	.	136
Bronze Sword, found on Haapa Kyla Heath, Nyland, Finland	.	136
Bronze Dagger, found on Winterbourne Bassett Down, Wilts	.	159
Section across Roman Road at Latchmore Green, Hants	*Facing*	164
Silting of Wor Barrow Ditch	.	212
A Typical Roman Road		*At end*

xv

CHAPTER I

INTRODUCTORY

THE more often we perform any action, the better we do it—and the less consciously. This is obvious from acts of daily life, such as shaving and dressing; we are able to perform these complicated actions almost automatically, so that meanwhile our consciousness is set free to think about other matters. Any attempt at conscious control will mar the success of the operation. Thus, when running upstairs, two at a time, who has not sometimes had a sudden misgiving and nearly stumbled in consequence? Similarly, when coming downstairs, in the dark in most cases, if the stairs are familiar we shall manage quite well, *if we do not stop to think*! We really know perfectly well when we have reached the bottom, but the very completeness of our knowledge renders it unconscious, and it is only a momentary scepticism which proves disastrous. We fail because we dare not succeed.

So, too, any new factor introduced, such as a new suit of clothes or a uniform, upsets us and makes us 'self-conscious' until the newness has worn off and we have become habituated to the new order. We then revert gradually to the unconscious perfection of perfect familiarity. Most of us for most of the time are half asleep and live by routine; it is only the unaccustomed which knocks us out of our groove and makes us, as we say, look facts in the face. What is true of the individual is true of the community. It is only some great event, like a hostile attack from without, which can stir great masses of people and make them co-operate intelligently.

The secret of this unconscious perfection is repeated performance. The man who acquired the habit of biting his nails when he was a boy bites them unconsciously when he is grown up and probably does it very well. The same reasoning applies also to all the specific functions for which our limbs are designed, such as walking. What, then, is the difference between a leg and a razor? They are both tools, the one for walking, the other for shaving. The only difference between them is that we have grown our shaving-tools outside our bodies instead of from within, and at a much later date. Consequently with the razor our performance is less unconsciously perfect, our touch is less sure than when we move our legs in walking. Also we have our legs always with us, and are necessarily always practising and improving our powers of using them.

Man has been defined as a tool-making animal. It would be equally true to define animals as tool-

INTRODUCTORY

growing men. The man who wants a trowel makes one out of wood and iron; but the beaver turns his tail into one.[1] The beaver's method is slow, but it is very sure: and it has this great advantage, that he is completely master of whatever tools he makes. It takes a long time to turn an ordinary tail into a trowel, and we may trust the beaver during the transformation to exhaust every trowel-like propensity inherent therein. But there are drawbacks to the beaver's method. For one thing, it has limits. No animal can be a walking bag of tools: he must as a rule make a few generalised tools serve many purposes. That is because he is limited in his materials to the substance of his own body.

There is thus amongst other animals no opportunity to accumulate capital, since the limb, and the power to use it as a tool to the fullest advantage, grow concurrently. We never see awkward animals, except the young who have not yet acquired full control of their limbs or the old who have lost it. Animals also grow only such tools as they can use, and they use none but what they have grown on their own bodies. Man was the first animal to grow a limb outside of himself by making tools out of wood and stone. This was a great achievement. In the first place, because it takes much less time, say, to make an eolith or sharpen a stake than to

[1] I am now told by naturalists that this is not so, but the illustration serves my purpose as well as others, such as the webbed feet of swimming birds, whose tool-like use is unquestioned. Perhaps the beak of a swallow would have been a more apt comparison.

grow canines or flatten your tail into a trowel. Moreover, once made and the principle grasped, however dimly, the external limb is capable of an infinity of modification, self-suggested by its very inadequacy as a tool. There is no time for automatism to set in before the possibility of fresh uses occurs, prompted sometimes accidentally by the tool itself. Again, each individual has consciously to make the tool for himself, and although this might become almost automatic after a time, complete automatism would be avoided by the desire to effect small, useful improvements, *and the ease and rapidity with which these could be produced.* Moreover, the external limb is not directly connected with the brain by a nervous system, like the fingers. The man is insulated from the arrow-shaft by the notched stone with which he is scraping it. Thus the vicious circle of automatism is breached. For all tools are slightly different from each other, and need intelligent control, according as they are used upon different materials. Also, one man may employ many kinds of tools, each a little different from the other, and therefore needing a different kind of control. This constant change is another safeguard against automatism, for attention is sustained and kept alert, watching each movement and consciously directing it. Again, the rapidity with which an external limb can be adapted to fresh uses causes it continually to run ahead of the power to use it, so that it always remains cleverer than its maker. That is what I meant

INTRODUCTORY

when I said above that other animals cannot accumulate capital. With men the desire outstrips the performance. The species of bird which is becoming a duck is always trying to make its feet a little more webbed than they are : but all the while it knows the exact limitations of its feet as propellers in water. If it had a man's brain it would attach some kind of leather paddle to its feet every time it wanted to swim.

There is thus added a third factor, intermediate between the man and his environment; so that

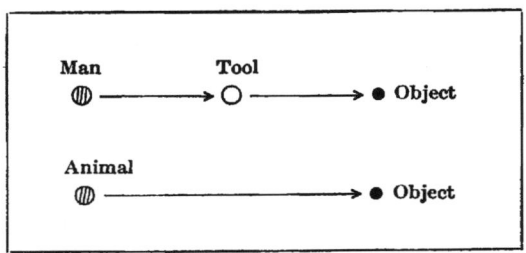

the different kinds of interaction between the two are multiplied enormously. The beaver alters his environment to suit his purposes, but he does so in a very wasteful and laborious manner by the *direct* action of his teeth and tail. Birds build nests, but they do it with beak and claw, not with any wooden nest-making tool. There is small scope for conscious intelligent action, because the tools in question are unchangeable throughout their lives, being parts of their bodies, and linked to the brain, the seat of consciousness, by a nervous system ; the limb-tools, therefore, learn their jobs so well that they never have to be prompted. Further, the mechanical devices of animals are mainly of a defensive nature and are almost always bound up with bodily structure, as, for instance, the fly-traps of orchids and the shells of oysters. Passive resistance is generally bad strategy in warfare; in the long run it is always by seizing the initiative that victories are gained. Camouflage by itself raises no man to the rank of hero.

The external limb, then—the first eolith—comes between man and his environment like a highly resistant substance in an electric circuit. So long as it is there the current of automatism cannot flow freely; from the resultant friction shines out intelligence; and the greater the friction the brighter the light. The power of intelligence grows with use, for it is quick to take a hint from its teacher the tool. The tool is improved, fresh demands are made upon intelligence to use the new tool aright, and so the process is continued, each in turn helping the other. Each step in advance was a small one, hardly won perhaps; but each step makes the next more easy. It may seem a far cry from the first generalised stone implement to the latest highly specialised aeroplane; but once the first step is taken the rest is comparatively easy. The aeroplane was implicit in the eolith. It has been achieved because there has been throughout no opportunity for automatism to take charge and put consciousness to sleep.

The invention of extra-corporeal limbs put a

INTRODUCTORY

stop to progressive structural modifications, for thenceforth such modifications took place *outside* the organism instead of within it as before. It is literally true that man survived by his wits; but that is also true of other animals. The difference lies in this, that, whereas (in the example I have taken) the beaver uses his wits to make his tool out of a bodily limb, man makes his by the quicker process of chipping a stone. Man's method has this enormous advantage, that from his familiarity with handling *things*, he can rapidly improvise new tools [1] to suit a new environment. He has learnt from his first efforts with sticks and stones to be quick to take a hint. He is therefore not nearly so much put out by a change in his environment. When the Ice Age overtook them, most animals grew fur; man adopted the shorter method of killing them and making their skins into warm clothes for himself and his family. The growth of his intelligence more than compensated for his loss of structural adaptability. Throughout the rest of nature, the price of survival is automatic obedience. Those who stop and question her authority are lost. Man started his career in a comparatively defenceless state, with no limb or part of his body specialised as a weapon of offence or defence. That perhaps was why he alone picked up and used the flints around him. With every other animal a changed

[1] I use the word in the widest sense, to include the defensive armour of clothes as well as offensive weapons and implements of all kinds.

environment involves a change of structure; slow changes in both are always taking place; but if the change of environment be too rapid the creature will not have time to alter its structure before it becomes extinct. It cannot change its ancestral beliefs in a moment; and it dies as a martyr in a losing cause. Thus perished the giant reptiles of the Jurassic epoch. How could it have been otherwise? One could hardly expect brains no bigger than a lap-dog's to make much out of such mountains of flesh.

We can now see why it is that the oldest crania of prehistoric man are so remarkably modern in their appearance. The specific human type from which we are descended was fixed once and for all at that time when the survival-value passed from man's bodily structure to his tools or extra-corporeal limbs. After that a change in the environment evoked but little response in man's body; instead, it stimulated his brain to invent new ' tools ' to counteract it. Further, man turned the tables upon nature and deliberately changed his environment by moving from one region to another, bringing ever fresh fields beneath his sway. Nowadays, when he finds himself in a malarial region, instead of learning to secrete an antidote, as any ordinary animal would in the course of ages, he swallows a dose of quinine which he has learnt to extract from a plant.

This method of procedure, however, has grave drawbacks. Man's body alone of all organisms is

INTRODUCTORY

permanently and irrevocably out of harmony with its environment. Man, in the person of his pre-human ancestor, intended to live an outdoor life, without clothes, getting his food daily by hunting for it : and he fashioned his body accordingly. That body is the legacy which that same ancestor has bequeathed to us and to our descendants, and there is no cutting off of the entail. We have to take it as it is, coddle it with clothes, shut it up in a house or factory, feed it unsuitably, deprive it of the exercise it requires, and use it to gain for us a livelihood as best it may. Use and disuse and changing circumstances since the palaeolithic period have modified it but little, and we are to all intents as much at home in our surroundings as a bull in a china-shop. Hence come the poet's plaints—the time is out of joint indeed when hands which might have belonged to a cave-man of Altamira draw only useless and ugly wall-papers that no one really wants or admires ! It is not only the soul that rises in us but the body which had elsewhere its setting and cometh from afar. We have created an environment which now grows almost in spite of us, and for which our bodies were never intended. We have burnt our boats behind us in becoming civilised, and our lives depend on the continued existence of a structure which may collapse at any moment. We in industrial Europe are like a colony of ants which has grown and multiplied away from the nest while continuing to depend on it for its food. If the chain of supplies is broken, it must rapidly perish of starvation. We are huddled too closely together, and there are too many of us. We *must* maintain the elaborate organisation of the system which has produced us; for without machinery and all that it implies we could not obtain enough food to support our top-heavy community.

I have said that the habit of manufacturing extra-corporeal limbs has grave drawbacks. But it has one advantage which compensates for them; it has preserved man's body in its primitive, plastic, unspecialised form, so that all the avenues of sense remain open. Each of the five pathways to the brain remain unobstructed and unblunted by special contrivances. That is because our primitive ancestor wisely refrained from rushing headlong into blind alleys, like his cousins the other proto-mammals. 'Some . . . became fleet of foot and developed limbs specially adapted to enhance their powers of rapid movement.'[1] Thus the ancestor of the horse, for example, sacrificed his five toes (which might have become fingers) and grew horny hoofs instead, thereby forfeiting for speed his chances of developing sensibility of touch. The proto-mammals

. . . attained an early pre-eminence, and were able to grow to large dimensions in the slow-moving world at the dawn of the age of mammals. Others developed limbs specially adapted for swift attack and habits of stealth, successfully to prey upon their defenceless relatives.

[1] Elliot-Smith, Pres. Address, Section H., Brit. Association, Dundee Meeting, 1912. *Report*, pp. 575-598.

INTRODUCTORY

Others took to the water or the air, and acquired the modifications in structure and manners of life necessary to accommodate themselves to their new environments.

Most of these groups attained the immediate success that often follows upon early specialisation : but they also paid the inevitable penalty. They became definitely committed to one particular kind of life ; and in so doing they had sacrificed their primitive simplicity and plasticity of structure, and in great measure their adaptability to new conditions. The retention of primitive characters, which so many writers upon biological subjects, and especially upon anthropology, assume to be a sign of degradation, is not really an indication of lowliness. We should rather look upon specialisation of limbs and the narrowing of the manner of living to one particular groove as confessions of weakness, the renunciation of the wider life for one that is sharply circumscribed (Elliot-Smith, p. 589).

Throughout the Tertiary Period our far-sighted ancestor ' lay low and said nuffin ', biding his time like Brer Rabbit. He did not, like so many, spoil his chances by giving way to fear on every possible occasion, he did not run away from danger on principle, and so have to adapt his limbs for swift flight ; nor yet did he yield to the temptation to clothe himself in protective armour. Nor did he cut himself off from the world by adapting nocturnal habits. On the other hand, he was not possessed by a devil of pugnacity ; he preferred vegetarianism to the horrors of carnivorous diet. Moderate in all things, he lived a life of meditative aloofness in the forest, waiting for something to turn up. His patience was rewarded ; what turned up was not any kind of external goods but the key to all such—an intelligent mind.

Man is the ultimate product of that line of ancestry which was never compelled to turn aside and adopt protective specialisations, either of structure or mode of life, which would be fatal to its plasticity and power of further development (Elliot-Smith, p. 590).

How did this happen ? Again I cannot do better than quote Professor Elliot-Smith's summary of his own address (p. 588).

The adoption of an arboreal life by some small insectivore-like creature, shortly before the dawn of the Tertiary Period, and its subsequent cultivation of the sense of vision . . . enabled man's remotest primate ancestor to escape from the domination of the sense of smell as the guiding influence of its life, and to cultivate its other senses, so as immensely to widen the sensory avenues by which the outside world could affect its conscious activities. The arboreal life, which demanded great activity and agility, led to the special cultivation of skilled movements of the limbs, and such an acquirement was clearly facilitated in this group by the perfection of visual control, without which finely adjusted actions of the hands and feet could not easily be learned. The acquisition of such skill in movement necessitated the increased perfection of the tactile and other sensory areas of the brain, so as the more nicely to control the adjustments and correlations of muscles essential for any precise action. Thus, we have a chain of linked influences that follow on the specialisation of the visual apparatus in the brain of our primitive arboreal ancestor—the perfecting of touch and the acquirement of skill in action. *The heightened acuity of vision and the expansion of the cortical area for storing visual impressions* [italics mine], together with the growing importance of touch, and in a less measure, perhaps, of hearing, immensely widened the psychical content of the life of the Eocene Tarsioid in comparison with that of its contemporaries ; but there is yet another factor which its mode of life called into play, which was fraught with the most far-reaching possibilities in the creation of Man. The co-ordination of large groups of muscles for the purpose of performing some precise action, which must be controlled during the stage of learning by tactile, kinaesthetic and visual impressions and memories—the fruits of experience—necessitated the formation of some cortical apparatus which would control and harmonize the activities of the various centres, regulating the muscular actions, and bringing the total sum of consciousness at any one moment to bear upon the performance of a given act. Out of such a necessity as this there sprang in the early ancestor of Man—and, though in much less degree, in certain other phyla also—an outgrowth of the motor cortex, which became the mechanism for attention and the orderly regulation of the psychical processes.

Now we are in a position to understand why it was that man, and man alone, has invented tools. He kept open all the channels of sense and developed each of them equally and none too much. Further, he acquired the power of associating and comparing the memories of impressions arriving through different channels. Thus, before leaping on to a branch it was necessary to assure himself that it was neither too big to grasp in the hand, nor too small to support his weight. This assurance he acquired by the use of his eyes, by looking before he leapt; but the memories by which it was tested, which contributed in each instance to form his judgement, were memories of touch—the associated memory of *bulk* and security, or the reverse. The sight of leafless, and therefore rotten, branches would arouse mistrust. Eventually he developed a power of co-ordinated control of complex muscular actions, a control which involved a high degree of intelligent direction. That is the crucial point in man's development. For at this stage ' the hand and arm are not only ready and free from the duty of progression, but they already have attained in great measure the skill and the cunning to perform what the intelligent will requires of them '.[1] Given a group of such intelligent animals living a semi-arboreal life on the margin of a forest-region; given an abundance of stones, preferably flints, lying about on the surface; add to these a highly intelligent animal, full of curiosity, and with hands free to pick them up and use them; and we then have the necessary ingredients of primitive tool-using man. It helps, but is not essential to our argument, to suppose that there may have been in progress at this stage a process of deforestation, caused perhaps by a climatic change. Then the conditions would be such as to encourage a wholly terrestrial existence. The restless hands, deprived of their ancient tree-craft, would be for ever picking at the new strange things upon the ground. They knew the feel of branches; they would soon grasp the uses to which sticks could be put.[2] They may have held and thrown nuts; they would then the

[1] Elliot-Smith, p. 594.

[2] The plate facing p. 16 illustrates for the first time what is probably the only known wooden weapon of the palaeolithic period, and the oldest wooden object of human manufacture that has been discovered. It is a pointed shaft of wood, 15¼ ins. long, and it was found in the *Elephas Antiquus* bed at Clacton-on-Sea, Essex. It is now in the collection of Mr. Hazzledine Warren of Loughton, Essex, to whom I am indebted for permission to reproduce the accompanying photograph. Mr. Warren adds the following descriptive note : ' Geologically the deposit in which it was found is to be

INTRODUCTORY

more readily appreciate the missile value of stones. Quick to take a hint from nature and from accident, man could soon learn not only to use such objects but to adapt them to his uses. Once the first step is taken, the rest is easy.

We see now why it was that man alone of all animals made tools. It takes two to make an invention, the man and the thing. Flints there always were in abundance, but it was not till Piltdown man, or some predecessor of him, came along that the first eolith was made. For flints appealed in vain to the already over-specialised creatures who were his cousins. Environment by itself can create nothing when the soil is unprepared. That is the explanation of so many geographical problems. It explains, for instance, why there never grew up any great native civilisation in the alluvial valleys of America, or in the 'Mediterranean' regions of that continent and Australasia. Nature was ready but man was not. The soil was not barren, but the seed had not been fertilised. Exactly how or why man in such regions fell short we cannot yet say; but we shall not be far wrong in supposing that his racial ingredients were not suitably mixed. The

---

correlated with an early part of the middle or 50-foot terrace of the Thames basin gravel. Abundant relics of human flint-work are found in the same bed; this flint-work is perhaps a little more suggestive of the Early Mousterian than of any other period; but it is unfortunately impossible to define its horizon exactly, as the flints consist for the most part of such waste débris as is found in the flint industries of all periods.'

Of course this actual wooden spear belongs to a period when the art of working stone had reached a high point of excellence.

cross between man and his environment was too wide to be bridged and the union was therefore a sterile one. The Australasian type, for instance, is too pure a strain to develop far: there is needed a constant and repeated mingling with other breeds, bringing with them new customs and ideas, to keep the vitality of intelligence keyed up to the highest pitch. In the old world of Europe and Asia this intermingling was constantly taking place, and in an environment which always rewarded effort. In Australasia the environment was there but man grew stale from lack of new blood from outside.

So, too, coal, water, and iron have always existed, but it was not till ' the appointed time ' that a man thought of bringing them together and making a steam-engine. Everything is implicitly present in everything else, but needs disentangling and re-assembling. This process is what is called progress.[1]

By inventing tools man was able to alter his environment to his needs. At first, no doubt, he did not effect very much, but the important fact is that the centre of gravity, so to speak, was shifted from the rest of his body to his brain, the organ of intelligence. For the first time, the intelligent

[1] Historians are divided into two schools according to the importance they attach to one or other of these two factors (man and his environment). The followers of Buckle and Ratzel regard the environment as more important. The other side, whose motto is that ' history is the biography of great men ', ignores the environment. The truth lies midway. The history of man, like that of other natural species, is a continual give and take between him and his environment. In primitive communities there is on the whole not much ' take '; in highly civilised ones there is a great deal. But there is present throughout a little of both.

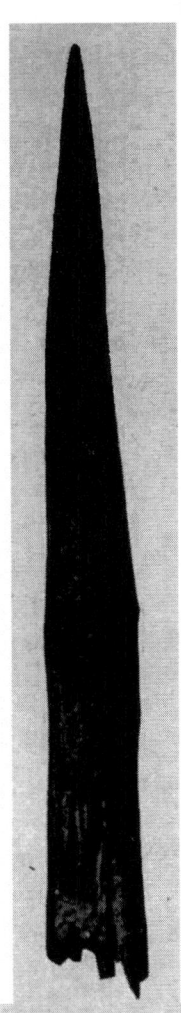

PALAEOLITHIC WOODEN SPEAR-HEAD.
Found at Clacton, Essex. (Scale about ⅓.)

Facing p. 16.

INTRODUCTORY

control of behaviour had a direct and paramount survival-value. Automatism, which is conservatism, was out-flanked. From that moment onwards knowledge became power. There were of course other factors in the development of man hardly less important than tools. Language is one of these and it must have greatly increased the powers of associative memory. Both handicraft and language contributed in developing the power of the brain and consequently its actual size. While the rest of the body remained almost stationary, the brain developed *pari passu* with the tools, each in turn helping on the other. The brain has thus literally grown at the expense of the body, and it has done so largely through the sense of touch—through the continual need of controlling the movements of the fingers and hands in making and using tools, and through a growth in the intelligent perception of the qualities of things which comes from constantly handling them.

In the course of evolution of the human brain there is added to this cortex of man's simian progenitor a mass of tissue, roughly, about five hundred cubic centimetres, bigger than the whole of the gorilla's brain; and as the sensory areas of the human brain are practically equal to those of the gorilla, all this enormous increase goes to swell the dimensions of those parts of the cortex which do not receive sensory impressions directly. These neopallial areas are at least six times as large in the human brain as they are in the gorilla's (Elliot-Smith, p. 594).

The close connection between tools and brain will now become clear. Primitive tools were the highest existing functions of brain made manifest. Like language they are the incarnation of intelligence. That, for an archaeologist, is the gist of the matter, and that is why he spends his time in studying them. All tools, of course, are not equally instructive. It would be wrong to judge the Englishman of to-day by his railways rather than by his aeroplanes. Moreover, what I have said applies more specially to primitive man than to his civilised relations. The use of writing and the growth of literature, both of them widen the field of our judgement. But even now we form our opinion of a man as much by those extensions of his personality, his clothes, as by his less tangible qualities : and clothes come well within the class of tools which the archaeologist studies. It is perhaps partly for this reason that we like to *see* any one whose books we have read, or whom we have known only by repute. The desire is a legitimate one ; for, after all, clothes are merely a kind of fur which we grow to protect ourselves from the cold. When once we have come to regard all those external contrivances which I have summed up in the word 'tools' as extra-corporeal 'limbs', as consciously devised extensions of our personality, then and not till then shall we understand what is the underlying factor in human evolution. It amounts to this, that by growing different kinds of external limbs men have developed into a vast number of different genera and species ! The old purely anatomical bases of race-classification are then seen to

THE MORTLAKE BOWL.

A typical vessel of the neolithic period, found in the Thames at Mortlake and now in the British Museum. Height 5·1 inches ; diameter 6·9 inches. (Scale ½.)

Facing p. 19.

be but the splitting of hairs. There is far more specific difference between the millionaire with his huge array of ' tools '—a microcosm in himself—and the crossing-sweeper with his broom and a few rags. The anthropologist of the future must, when he wishes to classify mankind, betake himself to the sociologist for his facts. This may seem fantastic, but is it really so ? Is it more fantastic to classify men by the kind of house in which they live than to classify snails by their shells ?

This brings us to the last stage of the argument. Tools are to the student of man what fossils are to the student of life in general. From them he learns what he can of the manners and habits of their maker. They are records of a most intimate kind, these *disjecta membra* which man has left lying about, these cast-off limbs of his extra-corporeal evolution. One can learn more about a vanished race by handling the things their hands have made, their pottery, their stone and bronze implements and their ornaments ; by walking along the roads which have grown under their tread ; by climbing the grassy slopes of their abandoned earthworks, or resting in the shadows of their mighty buildings ; one can learn more in this intimate way than by reading all the books that have ever been written. For the letter killeth, but the spirit still haunts their old handiwork, and one can absorb it by the mere contact. The true connoisseur will tell you nothing till he has touched the specimen you are submitting to him. It grew out of the mind of its maker through his fingers and back through them alone can it tell you its story.

The sense of touch is the most generalised and most fundamental of all the senses. The others are but specialised developments of the sense of touch. Our eyes feel the waves of light; our noses feel the particles thrown off; our ears feel the vibration of the air; taste is only an intense sensation of touching, with a little smelling added. It was through the sense of touch more than any other that man's brain developed: he literally felt his way through the dark glades of the forest out into the daylight of intelligence. His mind grew up as a pot grows beneath the potter's hand; and as the mind of man has developed in the past, so too should our minds be enabled to develop in each one of us individually. It is a law of nature that an organism can only grow to maturity by recapitulating the history of its ancestral development. It can only follow the road along which, in the person of its ancestors, it has already gone. It cannot advance more than one stage at a time; it cannot assimilate ideas too foreign to its state at any given moment. How does this apply to the theory of education? We have seen already that man's physical evolution came to a dead stop with the transference of survival value to his brain. From that point onwards the brain has gone on developing at an ever-increasing rate, interacting throughout with the sense of touch, which was the main factor in

INTRODUCTORY

its evolution.[1] Obviously, therefore, we should apply this to our methods of education. We should educate through the sense of touch. We should develop the power of our brains in the same way that we human beings as a species developed it in remote prehistoric times : and we should at the same time call into play that conscious co-ordination of hand and eye (and ear) which we saw went with the sense of touch and helped the growth of intelligence.

The facts of archaeology are therefore the raw material of education. This conclusion is irresistible when the facts are arranged in logical sequence. Intelligent behaviour depends on the power of co-ordinating our actions towards a consciously envisaged end. This depends on the power of evoking and using associated memories ; man is the only animal which has developed a part of its

---

[1] In case I have not made clear the trend of this part of my argument, I quote, from Samuel Butler's *Evolution Old and New*, a passage which gives the gist of it : ' The organ and its use—the desire to do and the power to do—have always gone hand in hand, the organism finding itself able to do more according as it advanced its desires, and desiring to do more simultaneously with any increase in power, so that neither appetency nor organism can claim precedence, but power and desire must be considered as Siamese twins begotten together, conceived together, born together, and inseparable always from each other ' (Edn. 1911, pp. 217, 218). Applied to primitive man this means that the desire to make tools and the power or skill in producing them have grown up together. He learnt how to make a stone axe by making it ; and the more he made the more dexterous did he become. But as his dexterity increased, so too did his desire grow to make even better axes than before.

The same line of reasoning applies, of course, to the other senses and to the power of co-ordinating them in the performance of skilled actions, like chipping a flint. But for the sake of clearness I am confining myself to the sense of touch. It was upon the work of the fingers that all the senses were concentrated.

brain to hold these memories; he alone can compare remembered impressions which have reached his brain through different channels of sense, and he alone can co-ordinate his muscular movements to perform an intelligent action based on this remembered experience. He has learnt to do so mainly by making 'tools', and has perfected his manual dexterity and the powers of his brain concurrently by means of continual practice. The brain of a child is like the brain of a man at the beginning of the stone age; according to the law of recapitulation it must develop along the same general lines as the brain of man has developed from then till now. To give an opportunity of doing this we must provide it with the same kind of materials as prehistoric man used to sharpen his wits on. There is however one qualification necessary. An organism which recapitulates does so, as the word implies, imperfectly and hurriedly; like an actor saying over his part, it needs a cue here and there, but may slur over passages with which it is familiar: they cannot, however, be entirely omitted, for they are themselves the cue to what follows next.

Our brains have grown by being used as instruments for dealing with refractory nature. While he was chipping the blade of his stone axe man was at the same time giving a keener edge to his own faculties. Throughout, the brain has developed through continual contact with the environment by means of the senses. Therein lies the full, complete,

INTRODUCTORY

historic vindication of visual, tactile and auditory methods in education. Provide the learner at the start with something he can perceive through his senses and he will at once get a grip of his subject. His brain will get hold of something to try its strength upon—a fact, sensorily perceived. Subjectively the effect will be to develop the power of his brain. To begin in any other way is like grinding without grain; the millstones revolve and rapidly wear themselves out; or like the racing engines of a steamer when the screw is out of water—because there is nothing but thin air to grip, the bearings get over-heated and the machinery is damaged.

CHAPTER II

THE HISTORY OF MAN

IN the last chapter I covered rather a large area of inquiry, and dealt with many questions of a highly speculative nature. I believe that the conclusions at which I arrived are correct, but it is not at all unlikely that many of my readers may disagree. I will therefore say at once that what now follows is largely independent of them, and does not necessarily collapse if some of the positions there taken up should be thought untenable. For the purposes of this book it is only necessary for the reader to admit the peculiar value of 'tools' to the student of man. I believe myself that this value is greatly enhanced if one admits the close connection between the evolution of tools and the growth of man's brain-powers. But, strictly speaking, it is only necessary to regard these 'tools' as art-products of a primitive kind, capable, therefore, of throwing light upon the nature of the men who made them. The truth of this will, I think, be universally conceded, and in fact it is the principle which forms the basis of all archaeological work.

The archaeologist deals with the works of man in the past ; it is through them that he is able to reconstruct a picture of the conditions which obtained at any given period, and to trace the evolution of culture.

If I were dealing only with the study of prehistoric man my task would now be an easy one ; I should proceed at once to describe some of the technical methods by which the archaeologist arrives at his results. But my aim is a more ambitious one. I wish to demonstrate that archaeology is only a special aspect—the time aspect—of the science of man in general; that archaeology, in fact, is the sister of history, and that both are the children of anthropology. If I were writing only for anthropologists I should not labour this point, for I should be preaching to the converted. Let me show this by quoting a description of the aims and content of anthropology which has been written by one of its leading exponents :

Anthropology is the whole history of man as fired and pervaded by the idea of evolution. . . . It studies him as he occurs at all known times and in all known parts of the world. It studies him body and soul together—as a bodily organism, subject to conditions operating in time and space, which bodily organism is in intimate relation with a soul-life also subject to those same conditions.

After showing that anthropology is the ' child of Darwin ', who gave it the breath of life, he continues :

With Darwin, then, we anthropologists say : Let any and every portion of human history be studied in the light of the whole history of mankind, and against the background of the history of living things in general. It is the Darwinian outlook that matters. None of Darwin's particular doctrines will necessarily endure the test of time and trial. Into the melting-pot they must go as often as every man of science deems it fitting. But Darwinism as the touch of nature that makes the whole world kin can hardly pass away. At any rate, anthropology stands or falls with the working hypothesis, derived from Darwinism, of a fundamental kinship and continuity amid change between all the forms of human life.

It remains to add that, hitherto, anthropology has devoted most of its attention to the peoples of rude—that is to say, of simple—culture; who are vulgarly known to us as 'savages'. The main reason for this, I suppose, is that nobody much minds so long as the darwinising kind of history confines itself to outsiders. Only when it is applied to self and friends is it resented as an impertinence. But although it has always up to now pursued the line of least resistance, anthropology does not abate one jot or tittle of its claim to be the whole science, in the sense of the whole history, of man. As regards the word, call it science, or history, or anthropology, or anything else—what does it matter? As regards the thing, however, there can be no compromise. We anthropologists are out to secure this: that there shall not be one kind of history for savages and another kind for ourselves, but the same kind of history, with the same evolutionary principle running right through it, for all men, civilized and savage, present and past.[1]

This admirable passage is inspired by the true spirit of science, which takes man as it finds him emerging from the society of other animals by virtue of his greater intelligence, and which follows him on his upward course through prehistoric and

[1] R. R. Marett, *Anthropology*, Home University Library, pp. 7 and 10-12.

historic times. This progress if at times slow is a continuous one, and the breaks in it which were once demanded by the theologian disappeared with the discovery of evolution. Man is a species whose activities past and present cover a wide range, and have now enlisted a large body of investigators. But whatever their particular line of inquiry, it is man and his works that they are studying; it is man and his works that give unity to all their various researches. Now, during the last half century or so, this idea of the unity of man has been steadily growing all over the world amongst thinkers, and amongst the ' working classes ', though it has not been glimpsed by party politicians or by the majority of scientific specialists. We need not discuss the case of the politicians, but we must consider the men of science for they are important. They are so, because they belong to the only living movement besides the labour movement which has any claim to be regarded as world-wide. How comes it, then, that the members of a world-wide movement are blind to so patent a fact as the unity of the human race in its struggle with nature throughout the world and throughout the past ? It comes, I think, from the fact that each one is too absorbed in his own specialism to take a wider view. But this weakness of vision is a very different thing from absolute blindness : it can be cured if the sufferer be caught when young, and can be entirely prevented by a proper education. Specialisation is necessary in all research, which cannot produce results without some subdivision of labour. But it is rightly mistrusted by many who fear the resulting narrowness of outlook. Is it really necessary thus to sacrifice our specialists on the altar of exact knowledge ? I think not ; there is a way out of the dilemma. I would have this unity of human life with that of other living creatures, and this unity of human endeavour throughout the ages, brought home to every man, woman and child that is capable of being educated. I would have the facts of history, prehistory, biology and geology so presented to them that they could not fail to draw from them the logical conclusions. I would have the names of the lessons altered in the time-tables, and the lessons themselves re-arranged upon a chronological rather than a geographical system. Mediaeval history should take the place of ' English history '—or, rather, that farrago of futilities which is usually so described. The connection should be shown between contemporary events in different countries. The natural curiosity of youth should never remain unsatisfied. Of regions, and peoples without a history, it should be definitely said that they have no history, and why—or if the cause be our own ignorance, it should be stated that this is so. The filling up of these gaps in historical knowledge is one of the main objects of archaeological research ; and it is in replying to questions about these gaps that the teacher can bring home to the pupil the way in which new knowledge is acquired.

I believe that history so taught will inevitably foster the idea of the unity of man.

The historical student, who has absorbed this idea and into whose very marrow it has penetrated, will henceforth look with new eyes upon history. He will see modern history as just one scene in an act which began in prehistoric times. He will envisage the whole as one continuous process. He will view all history (past, present and future) as the drama of man's struggle with his environment.[1] Let me quote an example. One of the most fascinating acts in this drama is the gradual taming, so to speak, by the agriculturalist, of an originally wild tract of country by the clearance of forests, the draining of marshes and the extermination of wild beasts. This process was begun when men ceased to live by hunting. It was inaugurated in remote prehistoric times by the first man who dug to make a garden or a field to grow wheat in. It still continues in the new world, but in an old country like England the battle is won, and fighting is confined to occasional skirmishes (of which the war-time ploughing-up of grass lands is one). In this process of the taming of wild nature, the gradual clearing of large areas of virgin forest plays an important part. The student whose outlook is anthropological— using the word in its widest sense,—who has a logical grip of his subject and who can select his

[1] Including, of course, other men. But this aspect of the struggle, which is war, is not likely to be forgotten, and has up to now had far too prominent a place in historical text-books.

material accordingly, will be sure to pay special attention to this question. For it gives a meaning to late mediaeval history by revealing that period as a culminating stage in a process which began in prehistoric times. Further, his researches thus inspired will give life to the dry bones of the past by bringing it into connection with what is going on to-day in America and elsewhere.

This stage of forest-clearing is of course only one stage in the history of man's conquest over nature, though it is an important one. In the ideal course of universal history it would be given its proper place. What, then, it may be asked, do you suggest as an ideal outline scheme of universal history?[1] It would be obviously impossible here to give a full and adequate reply to such a question. I must content myself with making a few suggestions which I should like to see followed up in more detail by some one with the necessary breadth of knowledge. Any such outline must be built up upon a logical framework of time and space. The *ultimate* unit of study and of teaching being man, not arbitrarily selected groups of men, an attempt must be made to give an account of the conditions which obtained in each period in every region of the world. By this I do not mean the names of the rulers or details of tribal warfare, but the general economic conditions, the ideals of the age and the level of culture as shown by the arts. The

[1] These words were written before the writer knew of Mr. Wells' *Outline of History*, which had not then begun to appear.

THE HISTORY OF MAN

danger of such a scheme is that it may lose its reality in vagueness; but this can be avoided partly by vivid accounts of the geographical conditions of the regions concerned, partly by a judicious mixture of correlated local history. By thus teaching local history as a part of universal history both will benefit. Universal history will gain definition through contrast, and by its association with familiar things will become real, and also, incidentally, more easy to remember. (There is a good psychological reason for thus beginning with sensorily perceived facts.) Local history, too, will be seen in its true perspective. The various episodes will either be relegated by the pupil as trivial, or will take their place as parts of a larger movement. It is no small part of the educative value of history properly taught that it strengthens the critical faculty by supplying touchstones for appraising facts, the test being their place in a process—in the last resort, their place in the history of human achievements. Obviously such facts as the reactionary forest policy of the Norman hunter-kings will appear more important than, for instance, the *cul-de-sac* of Monmouth's rebellion.

It is instructive to look by way of contrast into existing text-books of history, such as are used for teaching purposes. There are many obvious openings for criticisms, even if we accept them at their own valuation as national histories and no more. Selecting, for instance, the example I have given above, we may search in vain for any mention at all of forests and parks, though these had a most important place in the national economy as the ultimate sources of much of the meat, wool and clothing of the period. Nor do we find more than (occasionally) a bare reference to the part played by forests and forest-law in aggravating civil strife, like the Barons' War and the Civil War, though this fact is admitted by professional historians. But the text-books are fundamentally wrong in principle. They foster a narrow spirit of national patriotism, which if pursued to its logical end leads to a fiasco like that of Germany. There runs through them no thread of unity; they lead nowhere and end as lamely as they have begun, generally at the point where history begins to get most interesting. They select an arbitrary starting-point, after discussing the 'ancient Britons' in a few lines; they confront the student with a *fait accompli*—Britain at the first, second or third conquest usually—with barely a hint of the causes which preceded; and they inevitably convey the impression, either that all that happened before the Norman Conquest or the coming of Julius Caesar was of no importance, or else that it is a blank of which nothing is known. Both are of course wholly untrue; but the trouble is that these erroneous first impressions are too often life-long inheritances.

Text-books of history, in their present form, are a legacy from the past. They are modelled on larger works which were written (in an epoch of enthusiastic nationalism) before the discoveries of prehistoric man had been made, or, at any rate, before the new knowledge had penetrated into the historian's study. They are as a rule completely out of touch with current ideas, and are 'survivals', as functionless as the vermiform appendix, which may once have served some useful purpose. Worse than that, they are (also like the appendix) dangerous anachronisms, well calculated to jeopardise the fortunes of a project like the League of Nations, which, if it is to be of any use, must command a loyalty more deeply rooted than national patriotism.

It is not of course entirely the fault of the writers that the text-books are narrow in outlook and limited in scope. Their writers have to supply a demand which is regulated from without by examinations. But it *is* the fault of those who set the standard of these examinations. And yet, can we blame them? They were themselves 'educated' in the same way, and when their 'education' was finished they were only too glad to be quit for the rest of their lives of such 'history' as they had been taught. It is only a few enthusiasts who survive their school-days with the love of knowledge still unquenched. The fault is that this love, which is the mainspring of all research, is never presented to them as a desirable possession—nay more, is even tacitly condemned as unworthy, or at least as a trivial thing without the prestige of the conventional curriculum. And so the vicious circle continues, and it will remain unbreached until the spirit of scientific research penetrates our mediaeval system of education. For it *is* mediaeval, and represents roughly the sum total of existing knowledge at the time when universal education was adopted. The alterations since then are mere patchwork additions or corrections of detail.

The whole scheme of our historical education needs recasting to bring it into line with modern discovery and with modern political ideals. Education aims at producing good citizens, and it must therefore be in touch with the highest ideals of contemporary society, or it is dead and meaningless to those who come under its influence. It is untrue to say that the materials for such history do not exist. They exist in an almost bewildering profusion. 'It needs', says Mr. H. G. Wells,[1] 'but a change in the requirements of a few big examining authorities to cover the land with a mushroom-growth of books, wall-maps and diagrams suited to a saner teaching of history.' It needs also, of course, a change of heart on the part of those authorities—a real desire for something wider and better, and, if not the knowledge, at least the imagination to conceive the ideal and to appreciate its practical importance. 'A saner teaching of history', Mr. Wells continues, 'means a better understanding of international problems, a saner national policy and a happier world.' No truer words were ever written.

Now it should follow from all this that not only our education but also some of our learned societies

[1] *John o' London's Weekly*, April 19, 1919.

ought to be regrouped round this central subject of human history; those of them, that is to say, which deal with man, and which are represented in England by the Society of Antiquaries, the Royal Anthropological Institute and the English Historical Society. In the course of time some such coalescence will, I think, come, but as yet the time is hardly ripe for it. We cannot alter ideas and outlooks by altering the outward forms of organisation. The change must come first from within. Until the desirability of such a fusion is felt strongly by all the members—or all the effective members—of the societies concerned, it would be premature to suggest any such amalgamation. It would be only a change of name, if it did take place. One may regret, for instance, that the Society of Antiquaries pays so little regard as a society to the anatomical side of human evolution, but, after all, the work is done, when required, by some expert from outside, and not much is lost. What does give rise to very real regret is that individual archaeologists should sometimes take so narrow a view of their science as deliberately to disregard valuable anatomical evidence unearthed in the course of their excavations. That is the kind of lapse which would be impossible if the excavator's education had been conducted on the broader lines I have suggested—and the education of such an one would, of course, have been in this respect much fuller than the education of the majority.

Good as the modern expert undoubtedly is, he

would be none the worse, as a rule, for a somewhat wider range of interests; and he would probably be the first to admit it. His own special researches would be all the better if his education had been a more liberal one; and he would be a better man all round. Nevertheless it is thanks to him and his forbears that we now have at our command a great body of knowledge all ready and waiting to be edited and incorporated in the revised educational system of the country: and that is true not only of this country but of every civilised country in the world. It is here that the archaeologist comes in. If human history is to be taught as one and indivisible, we cannot do without him. What should we know of the civilisations of Crete and the Aegean, of the Hittites, of Egypt or of Mesopotamia, if there had not been archaeologists to uncover and interpret them to us? I need not labour this point: it is obvious if the premises are granted. If humanity is to be the central figure in the history of the future, everything pertaining to humanity will acquire a new value and a new interest for us. The results of the archaeologist will form part of the raw material out of which the educationalist of the future will construct his system.

'Human history is one history, and human welfare is one whole.' That is the justification for anthropology. That is why we anthropologists carry on with our work undismayed even in such times as the present. Indeed, now if ever is the time when our labours should reap their reward: for now for the first time mankind is deliberately attempting to unite in a single society. We alone can look without flinching on the break-up of old nations and civilisations, for we have assisted at the obsequies of too many to feel remorse. We have created mighty empires out of dust, and have watched them crumbling again. In our eyes a thousand years are but as yesterday. We deal wholesale in time; and having strengthened our vision by scanning the vistas of the past, we find that we can also view the future with less uncertainty. We may not be able yet, perhaps, to see far into it, but we have acquired the time-habit of mind, and that is what matters. We no longer live from day to day; we take long views.

The archaeologist has work to do for the good of the race; he is making bricks for the mansions that others after him shall build. That is his justification for devoting a lifetime to 'unpractical' pursuits. He may be wrong, but you will not lightly convince him of his error.

CHAPTER III

WHAT IS ARCHAEOLOGY?

THE subject-matter of archaeology consists mainly of pots and potsherds, stones, bones and earthworks. The archaeologist's principal implement is the spade. He is interested in the objects which are brought to light by digging, not because of any intrinsic beauty or value, but because they serve him as a means for attaining an end. They are the means by which he traces the evolution of man, both individually as one of a species and collectively as a member of society. Sherds and stones and such-like are used by the archaeologist because they are the only means available for the study of prehistoric man. They have, as we saw in the first chapter, a rather peculiar value in this respect; but it is mainly because of their almost indestructible nature that they are pressed into service. Could we call up prehistoric men and examine them like a Royal Commission we should attach less importance to these more material witnesses; though, even so, we should not neglect them.

It is important to grasp the fact that the sherds

WHAT IS ARCHAEOLOGY ?

and stones are only a means and not the whole end of archaeology. Nowadays one digs in the earth for knowledge, not for ' curios '. To our forefathers all objects of antiquity were merely ' curiosities ', or, at best, objects to illustrate recorded history, as it was then understood. Historical writings were the infallible guide ; and archaeological finds and earthworks had to be squared therewith. Thus it was that all the relics of all the races which had occupied Britain from palaeolithic times to the coming of Caesar were squeezed into a few centuries and labelled ' Ancient British '. Antiquaries accepted historical narratives and in the unaided light of them tried to explain the antiquities of every age. The idea of working in the other direction was quite foreign to them. To-day we test history by means of archaeology. We have successfully carried the methods of archaeology over the frontiers of history, and we intend to maintain there a permanent army of occupation. It would take too long to describe fully the way in which this revolution in method was brought about. The old point of view originated with the idea, common to-day amongst barbaric races, of the sacredness of the written word. It survived in the theological doctrine that the Bible contained an accurate and complete account of man's origin. It was the influence of this idea which caused dogmatic authority to be attributed to the written word of ' profane ' history. It, too, was ultimately responsible for the uncritical adherence given to statements in classical narratives, such as the Commentaries of Caesar. But the authority of Biblical narratives was shattered by the sensational discoveries of Boucher de Perthes, whose results proved beyond the shadow of a doubt that man was in existence long before the accepted date of the creation of the world. Geology assisted in the process, which culminated in the *Origin of Species*. The foundations of scientific archaeology in this country were laid by Lord Avebury, who, as Sir John Lubbock, introduced to England the work of Thomsen and the other Scandinavian archaeologists; and by General Pitt-Rivers, the first scientific excavator. It was the General who showed us how to reconstruct the past accurately and in detail by means of sherds and stones.

Unfortunately there are still many people who regard archaeology as the study of, or even the mere business of collecting, curiosities. Indeed it is, in this uneducated country, the popular view of this branch of science. That is not so true of Germany or America or of the small 'neutral' states, least of all of France. The other day I told a 'man in the street' that the Society of Antiquaries was going to excavate Stonehenge. Being for the moment off my guard, I was expecting him to share my enthusiasm. Not a bit of it. 'Oh, they won't do much good there,' he said. I was perplexed for a moment and asked him to explain. 'They won't find anything, will they?' he replied. That is the popular idea of an archaeologist's work, that he is engaged in a perpetual and usually fruitless search after some kind of buried treasure. To such an one the crowning moment in the career of an excavator would be the discovery of a large chest crowded with ugly but expensive jewellery, about a million years old. Mention to him Egypt—that poor, ransacked country of shoddy bric-a-brac—and his face brightens at once. Tell him, however, that you are interested in man's early struggles in all lands, and in your native country as much as in any other, and you will awaken no corresponding enthusiasm; you will rather encounter a politely veiled scepticism, and your researches will be regarded as the desultory efforts of a disappointed man who is making a virtue of necessity. The one question invariably asked of the intending excavator is, ' What do you expect to find ? '—a question expecting the answer (as the grammars say), ' Something worth a lot of money.' Of course what the excavator hopes to find—if he is a good excavator—is something which will enable him to date and explain the site he is excavating, or the period to which it belongs. Speaking generally, he hopes principally to find potsherds and other objects which from their position will enable him to date the site, and to say what people made it and for what object. Regarded in that way, the intrinsic value or beauty of the objects found is irrelevant.

This practice of making deductions from material evidence is not peculiar to archaeology. It is the method of Sherlock Holmes, of the military intelligence officer and of the student of living primitive races. It is equally applicable to people of higher culture, but has not been much used in the study of such people because other and easier methods are usually available. Countries which have developed a high degree of civilisation have usually preserved some written records of their past which are the special province of the historian or epigraphist. They have also usually been visited by travellers who have left contemporary accounts. Such, for instance, is the case in China, Japan, Central Asia and Abyssinia in the Middle Ages. Yet it is becoming increasingly apparent that the historian has now extracted from these written documents (whether native or foreign) most that is of value. It is to the archaeologist that one must look for the completion of the outline the historian has sketched.

I am, of course, quite aware that the deciphering of ancient scripts is usually regarded as the business of the archaeologist. But it is so special a branch, and demands such special knowledge and training, that it should rather be considered as a subject in itself. Epigraphy is to archaeology what palaeography is to history; both are indispensable to the master science of universal history, but they serve it in quite a subordinate capacity. A man may be a good archaeologist or historian and may yet be unable to decipher ancient records himself. It is usually impracticable for him to become an expert even in the script of a single country, which may, like Assyria, demand the work of a lifetime. It is in consequence impracticable for the excavator to master it completely. He can always get experts at home to do this part of his work; and in the leisure and comfort of the study they will do it much better than he could in the field. If this is not possible, then he must have an epigraphist on his staff. The actual business of deciphering is a whole science in itself, and has little or no connection with the science of archaeology. It is really no more the duty of an archaeologist to master it than it is the duty of a lawyer to acquire the skill necessary to engross a legal document with his own hand: and those who make life a study of epigraphy or palaeography are, in this respect, merely the scribes of an archaeologist. The excavator will be spending his time far more profitably if he devotes his early days to learning the elements of surveying, soil-study, photography and human anatomy, and the care and preservation of antiquities.

There is a wide, and as yet practically unworked, field of research open to the archaeologist in ' savage' countries like Africa. We know almost nothing of how this huge continent was peopled, or of the racial migrations which took place within it. Here the scientific excavation of ancient sites (which abound everywhere) will be most fruitful of results. Here, too, the interplay of history and archaeology can be beautifully observed.[1] History in such

[1] I use the word history here in its narrower sense of ' recorded history '.

lands is represented by the accounts of occasional travellers. Such accounts are as valuable to the excavator in Africa as the brief references of classical writers are to the student of prehistoric Britain. They are windows through which we can see, with the eyes of others, the living people whose remains we are daily bringing to light and handling. Up to now, men of science have rightly been too busy observing the living inhabitants of Africa to bother much about their history. But the time is approaching when they will exist no more in the primitive state, and then we shall have time to study their past. Meanwhile I would point out in passing that a good deal can be learnt by applying the methods of the prehistoric archaeologist to the study of such peoples. In the past there has been little synthetic study of modern primitive art - products. Above all, the geographical distribution of types has been somewhat neglected. By this I do not mean that observations have not been made of this distribution, but that good large-scale maps of small regions have not been attempted. Such maps would be invaluable to the prehistoric archaeologist because they would enable him to see the actual range amongst people living to-day of cultures which are still flourishing. They would give him an invaluable *point d'appui* for his own studies. He would particularly value information as to the range of trade and the methods by which it is conducted (whether from village to village or by long-distance pedlars). Unfortunately those who have travelled amongst primitive people and studied them have usually been anthropologists [1] first and prehistoric archaeologists afterwards—or not at all. There is needed a really good study of a primitive society by one whose primary interest is in prehistoric archaeology, and who would, therefore, devote himself to observing just those aspects which are most useful to the prehistorian—geographical and otherwise.

As an example of what may be called geographical anthropology I would quote the work of Mr. Henry Balfour, F.R.S., who has mapped the distribution of certain primitive instruments, such as the fire-piston and the musical bow. Such maps as these show the modern distribution of allied cultures, and throw light on the movement of people.

There is no essential difference in aims between anthropology (in the narrow sense of the word) and archaeology. With the important exception that the living subject is available only for the anthropologist the methods of both branches of the science are interchangeable. There is no sharp line between past and present.

An instance of the application of archaeological and anthropological methods to existing conditions may be seen in modern war. It is the object of every commander to discover by every means in his power all that can be discovered about the activities of an organised community—the enemy. He may obtain his information either through direct

[1] Here I use this word also in its narrower sense, of the students of the culture of living primitive people.

intercourse with living persons (agents, prisoners and deserters) or from documents, or from the evidence of air-photos. In so far as he obtains his information from living persons he adopts the methods of the anthropologist; both elicit by cross-examination—often in both cases subtly disguised—certain facts which are important to them. In so far as he relies on documents, such as captured orders and confidential reports, he follows the method of the historian. In so far as he studies air-photos, he is working on precisely the same lines as the field-archaeologist. In each case we need only substitute ' humanity ' for ' the enemy ' and the analogy is perfect. Nothing is more striking to one who has observed the increasing reliance placed on air-photos than the use of purely archaeological methods in interpreting them. All that an air-photo does is to show the earthworks and tracks of the enemy; it needs experience to interpret and classify them correctly.[1] So, too, we can learn much of the enemy by studying his habits, just as the anthropologist studies the customs of primitive people. If, for instance, persons are observed regularly visiting a spot it is obvious that there is *something* of importance there. Reference to an air-photo may show what it is. The soldier does not despise humbler scraps of ' archaeological ' information. He is glad of the cap or the shoulder-

[1] The value of air-photos in archaeology will be very great in the future. They can be used in discovering and making plans of ancient sites. They will be particularly valuable in teaching a class indoors the methods of field-archaeology.

badge retrieved by a raiding-party, for it tells him the regiment that holds that sector, and tells it in a way that cannot, like prisoners' tales, leave room for scepticism. From scraps of evidence like this all along the line the intelligence department can compile at regular intervals a map showing the distribution of enemy forces along the front. In the same way, and by using the same kind of evidence, the archaeologist can produce a series of maps of a given area, showing the different races which have lived there; and he has as keen an eye for the migrations of peoples as the soldier has for the movement of large bodies of troops behind the lines.

In one respect the archaeologist is happier in this respect than the soldier; he is practically untroubled by the works of camouflage that may mislead the other. True, he has to beware of forgeries; but camouflaged antiquities are comparatively easy to detect, and only rarely met with in excavation.

CHAPTER IV

ARCHAEOLOGY AND HISTORY

WE are now in a position to give a definition of archaeology in terms of its aims. They are to find out by every available means all that can be discovered about the men of past ages. Such a definition suggests the question—What is the relation of archaeology to history? Are they mutually exclusive? Or do they overlap? Or are they fundamentally different?

The functions of history have been described once and for all, for this generation at all events, by Professor J. L. Myres in a lecture delivered at Oxford in 1910.[1]

'History,' he says,[2] 'as an investigation of what really happened, is as thoroughly a science as geology, or botany, or any other non-experimental branch of learning. But as a science which selects from among the things which have happened the things which are of human interest; and regards only those things as being of interest which are seen to have been instrumental in bringing about the "present", History stands alone; or rather takes rank

[1] *The Value of Ancient History* (Liverpool University Press).
[2] P. 7.

among those other branches of knowledge, like the study of Art and Morals, which are concerned not solely with the discovery and record of facts, and the ascertainment of the relations between them; but also with the application of a standard of value. History is a science of observation, it is true; but it is also a critical science. Its standard is one of value as well as of relevance; it relates its facts not only to other facts, but to the judgement and to the service of Man.'

Further on in the same address he draws a distinction between the history of regions like Central Africa, which have throughout remained aloof from the main current of European history, and that of the Mediterranean which profoundly affected it. ' It is the kind of difference which we admit between this or that old man and our own grandfather.'

It would be impertinent for me to praise so admirable a description of the character of History. I will merely add a corollary. The history which is of no practical interest to us Europeans is, to the people concerned, by no means without value. Granted that they may not have reached a high state of culture by our standards, their history yet represents the attempts of those societies of men to ' live well ' (as Aristotle puts it) in the environment in which they found themselves. This is no mere academic question; it is one of vital importance to us who have taken upon ourselves the responsibility of educating alien races. Are we, for instance, to teach English, or even European, history to the inhabitants of India and the Sudan? If Professor Myres is right, surely we should teach

E

them rather their own history, since it is that which has made them what they are. But, it may be said, the importance of European civilisation as a phase of human development, and its present almost world-wide dominance, is a good reason for teaching it to every one. Perhaps, if rightly taught; but whether even so they will profit thereby is open to question. At any rate history, like charity, begins at home, with the known and familiar, and works outwards; with the present, and works backwards.

But many people, like the inhabitants of the Sudan, have no recorded history such as we possess, and few or no historical documents from which to compile it. Here archaeology steps in to supply some of the required information. By his own special methods the archaeologist can reconstruct the history of peoples who have had no historians, and of ourselves before recorded history began. History as thus put together by archaeologists is never of course quite the same as true history, any more than a mended pot is the same as one which has never been broken. Archaeologists' history must necessarily remain silent on many points that would be made clear by a contemporary historian. Archaeology

. . . may give us an outline of the conditions of material life, of the arts and manufactures, warfare and commerce; of the masses of the population, and also, with good luck, of the minority who live in kings' palaces; it will measure ups and downs of national prosperity so far as imports and exports can measure them, of national morality so far as honesty in workmanship, or exchange, is a clue to that ; of the standard of taste, so far as this is expressed in decorative art employed upon some durable material. But it will necessarily fail to distinguish the fool from the sage ; the poet, or the prophet, or the patriot, from the prodigal, and the man with the muckrake. The last in fact will be, if anything, the most conspicuous of them all ; for his goods, at all events, cannot follow him where he is gone ; but remain to divert the archaeologist.[1]

But archaeological history is at any rate reliable ; or in cases of conflict archaeological evidence must always be decisive.

We thus see archaeology acting at one time as the handmaid to recorded history, at another as mistress of the house. In the early days of man in Europe, and until quite recent times in some other regions, archaeology is sole arbiter ; elsewhere she is subordinate but possesses a casting vote.

This vote is being used freely by the students of Saxon archaeology in England to check the statements in the Anglo-Saxon Chronicle. As an example of good work done in this direction may be cited the writings of Mr. E. Thurlow Leeds, of Oxford, and Mr. R. A. Smith of the British Museum.[2] Through these purely archaeological investigations several conclusions have already been arrived at. In addition, archaeological evidence has confirmed, amongst other things, the sites of the Battles of Charford and the Lea.

[1] *The Value of Ancient History*, p. 21.
[2] Articles in the *Victoria County History*.

Apart, however, from this use in checking recorded history, there is a great difference in value between archaeological objects belonging, say, to the Dark Ages, and those of the prehistoric period. For the Dark Ages are lit, if only faintly, by the light of history, but before them is that utter darkness which goes before the dawn. Hence, for our knowledge of the one we depend mainly on historical evidence, such as chronicles and charters ; while for our knowledge of the other we depend absolutely upon what we can extract from archaeological sites and their associated remains. That enormously increases the value of prehistoric over mediaeval antiquities ; for they are literally all the history we possess of the periods to which they belong. How to make them tell their story is the special business of the archaeologist, and will be described in the following chapters. But meanwhile I wish to emphasise this difference in value as strongly as possible, for often it is not realised even by museum curators. One will find show-cases lavished upon ' old ' and generally ugly china, while a prehistoric urn of a thousand years before the beginning of history is stowed away in a dark corner. There is no comparison between the scientific values of the two ; the one, if it be not beautiful, is worthless in such quantities except to the technical student of modern ceramics ; the other is a priceless and original historical document.

A word which might well be applied exclusively to those who confine their attention to the archaeo-

ARCHAEOLOGY AND HISTORY

logical objects of full historical times is the word 'antiquary'.

Let me briefly summarise the foregoing paragraphs before proceeding.

History is that which explains to every community of men how it has come to be what it is. History tells us of the deeds of great men as well as of the common herd. Where history is silent or as yet unborn we turn to archaeology to correct the outlines or cover the canvas. The value of archaeological material is greater or less in proportion to the absence or presence of historical evidence proper.

Finally, I would guard against a misunderstanding of my thesis. Because in moments of expansion I may fuse archaeology, history and even part of geology together and call the result 'human history', it must not be thought that I wish to create a new department of research. The change I advocate is, as I said above, a change of spirit and not of working organisation : though that may follow in due course. I think the student of each will profit by realising the place of his respective hobby in the synthesis of human evolution—the geologist, if he responds to the tense human interest which vibrates in the concluding stages of his record—the archaeologist if he perceives the futility of antiquarian dilettantism — the historian if he gains a broader outlook. Moreover, knowledge itself will gain if the issues be thus defined. At present there is a real danger that the indiscriminate amassing of materials will by its sheer dead-weight retard the rate of progress. For the prehistoric periods we need every scrap of evidence, for we can rapidly assimilate the little that comes our way and there is no danger of satiety. But that is not so with the historical periods. Of some periods we already have a picture of photographic accuracy. Let all original documents be preserved, by all means, but let them be buried deep in the storerooms of national libraries; and let not the student lightly disturb their slumbers. Already we are beginning to suffer from a surfeit of trifling articles, nine-tenths of which lead nowhere and are as tedious and unnecessary as the extravagances of lawyers' English. Let any one who doubts this consult the contents of our leading historical journal, or of the corresponding journals of most other countries for that matter, and if he can find ten per cent per annum of really valuable contributions to knowledge I shall be glad if he will send me the name of the journal in question. And why is this so? Because we have sacrificed our divine right of selection at the altar of the omnivorous idol we have created in our own likeness; because not only have we said, ' All historical facts should be preserved because they may be useful to some one sometime ', which may be true; but have gone on to say of any and every happening, ' This is a historical event and therefore it is worth talking about '—which is neither true nor logical.

Of course the whole question depends upon what

we consider useful and valuable. Here I stand with Professor Myres; but whatever our opinions, let us have *some* scheme, *some* standard of values of our own to test the ore by. It may interest some persons to know whether Disraeli was born in Bloomsbury or Islington; but really they should not write to the papers about it. It would interest many of us, mildly, to know whether Caesar landed at Dover or Deal, but that knowledge may be bought at too high a price.[1]

No one with a proper sense of the dignity of human history will waste his time and energy on such portentous trivialities.

[1] And even then we may be told later by the discoverer that he has changed his opinion !

CHAPTER V

ARCHAEOLOGY AND ANTHROPOLOGY

'WHAT, after all, is History', said the late Sir Edward Tylor, 'but a subsection of Anthropology?' Such a comprehensive view of the content of anthropology was natural in the father of that science, but, as we have seen, it is rather less than the truth, and does not do full justice to history.

Archaeology also, like history, comes theoretically within the sphere of anthropology, which, as Dr. Marett says, is the whole study of man. But in practice anthropology (excluding for the moment human anatomy) is mainly confined to the study of existing primitive races. We may therefore regard anthropology as consisting of three main phases—the earliest phase, which deals with the dawn of man upon the earth, the short culminating phase of history, and the present phase of living people. That all three are but phases of the central subject, Man, is admitted by all except the historians, and might well be admitted even by them without loss of prestige, subject to the qualification mentioned above. What practical results would follow from a universal admission of this unity? In the first place, it would follow that every student should have some acquaintance with each phase of his subject, instead of, as at present, with one only, or two at the most. The historian would benefit from studying the fundamental ideas of primitive culture, and from an examination of the background of his picture. The archaeologist would see many of his difficulties resolved, if he knew something of the psychology and habits of ' savages '; and he would be more readily able to appreciate the rate and methods of cultural development if he knew a little history—to which, after all, he is writing the prologue. The anthropologist would gain all round, by realising which kind of problems he can most help to solve, and upon which points, therefore, he should concentrate most attention. In fact, every one would gain, including the readers of scientific literature!

This breadth of outlook should be acquired early in life, before the period of specialisation sets in; and it should be acquired by all who wish to be considered well educated. Such an ideal is not as formidable as it may seem, and as the champions of the existing system will doubtless maintain. It is far less laborious than gerund-grinding, and far more easy to teach, because it is a living thing. Wealth of detail is not required, nor the memorising of any facts beyond the few which are necessary as guide-ropes.

We have considered archaeology, and found that it deals with man at all times throughout the past, but more particularly in prehistoric times; and we found that history takes up the tale where it is left by the archaeologist and carries it on up to the present day; and that in one respect the historian is greater than the archaeologist. We have found also that both are theoretically parts of a single science, anthropology, whose subject is man. But anthropology, as I said above, has a special province of its own, the study of the primitive culture of living people. There is then a distinction between the theoretical content of anthropology as described, for instance, by Dr. Marett,[1] and its practical content as evidenced by the actual researches of individuals. From this double use of the word there results a certain confusion of thought. It would be a good thing, I think, if some such word as 'andrology' were adopted for describing that synthesis which consists of archaeology, history and anthropology, the last word being confined to the sense in which it is now most generally used. Anthropology in this narrow sense would then be to andrology what the study of human anatomy is to zoology, or zoology in turn to biology —a part of the whole. But such verbal differentiations, though conducive to clear thinking, are not important when once the essential aspects have been seen. What *is* important is that, to nine people out of ten, anthropology now means skulls and folk-lore rather than the whole history of man!

[1] *Anthropology*, Home University Library, quoted above on p. 25.

While it must always be that the actual work is done in each case by specialists, it is an open question how far the results should be separately published. In other words, to what extent should the working organisation of research tally with its theoretical, philosophical arrangement ?—for that is what it comes to ultimately. Practically, the question has been answered already, by each nation after its own fashion ; and any change must come from below, democratically, in response to a generally recognised need. In England there is a fairly wide gulf fixed between archaeology and ethnography. The Society of Antiquaries, whose national pre-eminence is unquestioned, publishes no anthropological papers, and the *Journal* of the Royal Anthropological Institute contains only a very few archaeological papers. Taking as a test the contents of three numbers of the latter chosen haphazard and containing in all thirty-six articles, only six, or 16 per cent, deal with archaeological subjects. In a couple of contemporary numbers of the *Proceedings* of the Vienna Anthropological Society, out of twenty-eight articles, eleven are archaeological —nearly 40 per cent. In the Berlin *Zeitschrift*— perhaps the leading ' andrological ' journal of the world — both archaeological and anthropological articles are pleasantly mixed.[1] It is clear, too, from the character of the articles, that Continental students

---

[1] The percentage of archaeological articles in Vol. 38 (1906) is 36. I take this volume as I happen to have it in the house at the moment.

have as a whole a wider outlook on their subject than their British colleagues. I confess to liking the mixture of ancient and modern that I find in turning over the pages of the *Zeitschrift* and *L'Anthropologie*. It is agreeable and instructive to find in the same volume illustrations of palaeolithic wall-paintings side by side with those of the Bushmen, each described by an expert. Specialists are thereby forced to notice, if not to read, what would otherwise probably be overlooked. That is bound to react favourably upon them, in however small a degree.

In passing I would call attention to another respect in which Continental journals compare favourably with ours. More attention is paid to what might be called the application of anthropological methods to home affairs. I mean such subjects as the study of existing types of homesteads and farms and of their historical origin— the distribution of a certain type in certain regions, correlated with some racial or cultural factor. That is a branch of study much beloved by the Teuton. In France it has been seized upon by the anthropogeographers of the school of Le Play and Desmolins, represented to-day by Brunhes. And it is a peculiarly archaeological subject in every way, though demanding, of course, geographical treatment, like all other archaeological matters. It is the business of the anthropologist to apply his methods to the material at his own doors, just as much as to that which lies in far distant lands and amongst more crudely primitive people. It is his object to throw light on the past by studying its existing survivals; and it should be immaterial to him whether those survivals are remote or close at hand. Nay more, he should if anything pay more attention to those at home, for they are more likely to help in certain matters. We are more likely to unravel the origin and early stages of the development of a European custom by studying its survivals in the environment in which it has evolved than by studying a somewhat similar phenomenon in a different—perhaps tropical —environment. *Different* causes sometimes produce like results. (I am speaking now of *material* survivals, remember.) In the *Proceedings* of the Vienna Anthropological Society above referred to, out of twenty-eight articles, three (10 per cent) deal with anthropogeographical subjects of this kind: whereas out of all the thirty-six in the *Journal* of the Royal Anthropological Institute not a single one comes under this heading. And one may search the back numbers of *Archaeologia* almost in vain for any. The proportion of such anthropogeographical articles is in fact, in the Vienna *Proceedings*, exactly the same as the proportion of articles dealing with human anatomy, and this last is itself three times as great as in the British journal. So that it may be concluded that the Vienna people, as shown by the articles in their *Proceedings*, are equally interested in anthropogeography and human anatomy, and, by comparison with the English journals, three times more interested in both.

The importance of this particular matter—the study of primitive homesteads of living peoples—was forcibly brought home to me whilst excavating an ancient site in the Sudan. It happened one day that half of the modern village near which I was camping was burnt down. As the huts were only made of straw, it was not so serious a disaster as it may sound. I was very much struck, when visiting the scene of the fire, by the appearance of the ground. There were the pots and querns standing exposed on the hard earthen floors, and looking exactly like those I was laboriously uncovering close by! What made the resemblance still more striking was the presence of a fine pot of burnished red ware, ornamented with white-filled incised decoration. It was clearly a ' foreign ' importation, and the owner told me it came from a village some twenty miles farther up the Blue Nile, where pots of this type were manufactured. An exact parallel to this was the discovery of two imported red-ware pots low down in the site I was then excavating.[1] A careful large-scale plan of such a native village, made by some one who knew it intimately, would be of immense value to an archaeologist, especially if he was excavating ancient sites in that neighbourhood. But it is an anthropologist's job to construct one. Such a plan would derive a good deal of extra value

[1] See p. 74.

from the insertion of additional information which is denied to the archaeologist in his work — the sheikh's hut, the village bazaar, the shrines, women's quarters, cattle-sheds, etc., etc. It is precisely these explanations from living witnesses that give anthropological descriptions their peculiar and pre-eminent value : and in proportion as archaeologists come to work more and more with maps and plans they will demand corresponding map-work from the students of living peoples. Further, they will even find time to construct such plans during the brief intervals of excavation, and when funds are low.

There is another side of anthropology which is concerned with the anatomical study of the human body. This aspect is poorly represented in all the leading anthropological journals of Europe, the lowest percentage being again that of the *Journal of the Royal Anthropological Institute*. It is essential that an archaeologist should realise the importance of anatomical research and its bearings on his work, and to do so he must know something about it himself. He should at least be able to distinguish a human bone as such when he digs it up. The detailed description of skulls and other bones is the business of the human anatomist, and had better be left to him. The archaeologist, however, will profit in many ways by improving his anatomical knowledge, especially of skulls. For upon such a basis rests the whole structure of modern ethnology. It is, however, too intricate a subject for the archaeologist to follow up in all its details. The ideal minimum is the kind of knowledge required for the Oxford University Diploma in Anthropology.

By thus relegating human anatomy to the background, I do not wish to appear to underrate its importance; very far from it. But its very importance makes it a special subject, which the doctor and the comparative anatomist are, by their training, best qualified to study.

CHAPTER VI

THE METHODS OF ARCHAEOLOGY

IN these islands culture had already advanced from zero-point to a comparatively high level when we first encounter it in history. The successive stages are now nearly as certain and as clearly recognised as the different types of fortresses and earthworks in historical times. That is a fact that is little known, apparently, outside the ranks of specialists. A man may pass through school and college and still regard history before Caesar as a series of comic scraps between painted ' Britons ' and their environment, which usually consists of impossible Jurassic monsters. The Battersea shield and the Birdlip mirror are unknown to him ; and they are hardly the work of savages. But it is rather the absence of any perspective behind Caesar that is to be deplored. It is all the more necessary, therefore, to explain how this perspective can be acquired, and how archaeologists build up a chronological system without any dates.

The framework of this system is supplied in Europe by the development from primitive forms of certain objects made and used by prehistoric man, notably axes, knives, spears and pots. It would be impossible here to give any detailed account of the development of any of these. The reader must consult such works as Sir John Evans' *Ancient Stone Implements* and *Ancient Bronze Implements*, Canon Greenwell's article on the evolution of the spear-head [1] and Lord Abercromby's book on Bronze Age pottery. In these works the development of the different objects is traced, stage by stage, from the simple original to the many complex forms which were evolved from it in the course of ages. The bronze axe, for instance, which was originally made flat, in imitation of the stone axe, later developed side-flanges and a stop-ridge and finally a socket. These changes must have taken a long time to come about. Sir John Evans attempted to estimate the length of time in years, and many attempts have been made since. It is not, however, essential to reduce the series to terms of absolute chronology, though this must always be our ultimate aim. For even the provisional adoption of some system of absolute chronology is a great help to clear thinking. What is essential is to acquire the art of thinking in types instead of years, and to remember that the period of flat bronze axes precedes that of socketed axes by at least as many centuries as the Norman Conquest precedes the present day.[2]

[1] *Archaeologia*, vol. 61, 1909, pp. 439-472.
[2] I should add that in every such case the limits of a single modern nation are far too restricted for a proper survey of this material.

THE METHODS OF ARCHAEOLOGY

It may be asked—how do you know that the earlier types were not still in use at the time when the later ones had been developed ? We know this because the later types are *never found in association with* earlier ones ; or, more accurately, if there are four successive periods, A, B, C and D, the remains of A and B will be found together sometimes, those of A and C rarely, and those of A and D never.

We can now advance another stage and discuss the subject of *association*. An object is said to be found in association with other objects when these appear to have been similarly associated with it at the time of original loss or concealment. Association proves the contemporaneity of types. During the Bronze Age hoards of implements and weapons were often buried by pedlars and bronze-founders, and in many cases the place of concealment appears (fortunately for us) to have been forgotten. These hoards are of the greatest archaeological value, for they prove the contemporaneous use of the objects concerned. All the objects found in a given hoard are said to be found ' in association ', provided, of course, that the hoard has not subsequently been disturbed. Naturally, the

---

National areas are often convenient in carrying out the preliminary detailed research, in collecting materials for a corpus and so forth. But when it comes to interpreting the results and arriving at general conclusions as to the origin of cultures and the migration of peoples, it is impossible to pay any regard to such arbitrary and recent delimitations. This fact soon becomes obvious to the student of prehistory, and is of immense value in widening his outlook and sympathies beyond the narrow frontiers of nationality.

hoards themselves are the products of a specialised industry—that of the bronze-founder; and it would help us considerably to be able to equate them with other remains of the same period, such as, for instance, the barrows that were the burial-places of the dead. These burial-mounds, by their very numbers, form one of the most valuable classes of our evidence.

To make this process of equation by association quite clear I will take a few instances. They all depend upon the formula that if $A=B$ and $B=C$, then $A=C$, the sign of equality signifying contemporaneity. Associated in hoards with bronze implements, there have been found certain twisted gold armlets called ' torques '. In one case a torque of this type was found in a barrow near Christchurch in Hants.[1] In this instance, unfortunately, no pottery was found, but the conditions of the discovery make it at least very highly probable that the barrow in question was of the same period as others near by where cinerary urns of a well-known late Bronze Age type have been found. This, therefore, constitutes almost absolute proof that this very large class of barrows and cinerary urns was contemporary with the bronze implements of hoards like those in which gold torques have been found. We can assign both hoards and barrows to the same period. Other lines of evidence point in the same direction.

In many cases hoards of bronze implements

[1] *Proc. Soc. Ant.* 2 S., xxiv., 1911-12, pp 39-49.

were buried in an earthenware vessel. Too often, owing to the casual way in which all hoards have been discovered, the navvy finder destroys the pot, and by the time the discovery is made known all traces of it have disappeared. I know of very few absolutely authentic cases where even fragments of the containing vessel have been preserved. One of these was a hoard of socketed celts found at Worthing in 1877. The hoard is unfortunately separated now into three portions, preserved in the local museum at Worthing, the Pitt-Rivers Museum at Oxford, and the British Museum. With each portion are fragments of the pot in which it was found. If these fragments could be even temporarily brought together in the one place for examination, we should be able to restore, if only by means of measurements and drawings, the outline and shape of the original pot. So far as I know not even the separate fragments have been illustrated in any published account. It is a most interesting piece of research which is waiting for some one to undertake it, and it would provide us with a valuable clue to the pottery used by the people who made the implements. We should be able to equate with certainty two most valuable classes of evidence for the period —pottery and implements.

Another principle of archaeology is that of *stratification*. It occurs under certain conditions of soil and climate in any site that has been continuously occupied for any considerable length of time. It takes place in caves and in regions where the houses are of mud, especially where there is a period of summer rainfall. Unfortunately it does not appear to have taken place in England in the regions which were most thickly inhabited in prehistoric times, probably on account of the temporary nature of pastoral settlements. The value of stratification lies in this—that we are able to state definitely that, where two or more layers are found one above the other, the one which occurs at the bottom, with all the objects associated together in it, is the oldest, and those found above it are successively later : provided, of course, that the soil has not been disturbed after its deposition. We have thus an additional line of evidence to prove the relative ages of different types of pottery, implements and the like, quite independent of any internal evidence derived from a study of the objects themselves and their development. Indeed, when it is available, the evidence of stratification is to be preferred to all other classes of evidence, because it constitutes absolute proof. It is upon stratification that the science of palaeontology is founded.

The analogy in this respect between archaeology, on the one hand, and geology and palaeontology on the other, is a striking one, and is worth considering. Geologists study the history of the earth's surface, and palaeontologists trace the development of the different forms of life whose remains are found in stratified rocks. If archaeology is humanity revealed by its works, palaeontology is life revealed by its own remains. The aim of the palaeonto-

THE METHODS OF ARCHAEOLOGY 71

logist is to trace the development of living forms from their earliest occurrence down to the present day, at which point he hands over to the student of zoology and animal anatomy.[1] His methods are determined by the nature of his material, generally fossil bones. In a country like England, where we have an almost unbroken succession of stratified sedimentary deposits, we can trace the development of living forms with admirable clearness. We know that those forms which are found in the lowest strata must be more ancient than those which occur in the higher strata; and we can trace the origin, development and final extinction of unsuccessful species. In addition, we can select certain specialised forms which are confined to a comparatively limited span of existence, and we can use them to date other strata in other regions. Such 'typical fossils' are, for example, Micraster, Actinocomax, Holaster, Marsupites, which have been used to subdivide the chalk of southern England into zones.

It will thus be evident that the sciences of archaeology and palaeontology are built up on an elaborate structure consisting of the classification of types in chronological sequence. The aims of

[1] When I speak of the geologist being concerned with this or that aspect, I do not for a moment wish it to be understood that I would thereby exclude him personally from the study of other aspects as part of his subject. I merely wish to introduce a certain theoretical scheme of classification, based on fundamental realities, and by so doing to put in their right perspective certain aspects which have hitherto been neglected. This neglect results in a narrow and truly unscientific outlook which is often characteristic of scientific specialists. The specialist does not *really* know his own job if he knows that and no other.

both are to provide as many as possible of what may be called 'type fossils'—that is, simple but common objects whose relative (and, when possible, absolute) age is known. Absolute age in archaeology is rare, and for periods earlier than about 600 B.C. rests ultimately all the world over upon Egypt and Mesopotamia. A system of relative chronology can be established by excavation in any country that has been long inhabited, but it is left hanging in the air until linked up with Egypt, whether directly or indirectly through a third region. It is like a trigonometrical network set up in the heart of a newly discovered country. It is complete and perfect in itself, but unless it be connected up with some other system, or unless an astronomical reading is taken, we cannot place the network upon the map of the world. A single link is sufficient to make connection with the chain of organised knowledge.

It is important to realise what a complicated system this chronological scheme is. One is often asked, 'How do you know the age of such and such an object or site?' It is difficult in such cases to give a clear reply which will also be brief. Our chronology is like an engine, where each part has no meaning except in relation to another part. To understand the function of a single part one must know the whole machine and its workings. So it is with archaeology. To appreciate fully how and why it is possible to date an object or a site, one must see as a whole both it and the systems with

THE METHODS OF ARCHAEOLOGY 73

which it is connected. I will give an instance of this to make my meaning clear.

A certain ancient site, which we will call site A, was being excavated in the Sudan. We knew nothing about its age except that the topmost layer of the three stratified deposits could not be earlier than about 900 B.C. This date was obtained from the discovery of an Egyptian scarab with the name of a certain Pharaoh engraved upon it; a few other Egyptian objects of the same age were found subsequently and confirmed the genuineness of the discovery. Before this, we had only a relative system of chronology, without a single connection with the outside world, and we could not really say whether the series ended a hundred years ago or several thousands. But the discovery of the scarab enabled us to give an absolute date to the top layer and to all the objects found in it. Amongst these was a certain type of pottery of a reddish colour, made locally from gritty, granitic clay, and ornamented with incised decoration applied *after* burnishing and drying, but *before* baking.

Later on, a new site, which we will call site B, was discovered on the Nile about 25 miles away, and excavations were begun upon it. To begin with, we knew nothing whatever about it except that there was a large artificial mound covered with potsherds of a hitherto unknown type. With the exception of the site just described above, not a single excavation had been made within 500 miles of the place, and archaeological knowledge can hardly be said to have existed there. After excavations had been in progress for some weeks we were able to establish a relative sequence of types (mainly pottery vessels and sherds), but we had no clue to their age in years, though, of course, we had our theories. One day there was found, in the bottom layer of all, the entire remains of two pots. They were not made (like the rest) of soft Nile mud baked hard, but of precisely the same gritty clay as those in the top layer at site A. The ornament was similar and applied in the same way. It was evident that they had actually been made at site A during the top layer period (about 900 B.C.) and exported to site B, but as they occurred in the *bottom* layer at B, it was clear that the bottom layer at B was contemporary with the top layer at A. We thus had a date in years for this bottom layer, and we were able to say that the site was first occupied about 900 B.C.

That is how the chronological systems of archaeology are built up. It is obvious that the further removed we are in space from the country which supplies us with our absolute chronology, the more approximate will our dates become. That is why it is so difficult to give any absolute dates to the prehistoric periods in Western Europe. A chain is no stronger than its weakest link. There is room also for marginal errors in each of the many stages, and the error is liable to accumulate. The succession of types, and therefore of periods, remains firmly established in the light of fresh discoveries.

In spite of this, however, our approximations in the long run get nearer and nearer to the truth. We advance all the while in an upward curve, though there are dips in its upward progress.

It may be asked—how do you know one type of potsherd from another? Did not the people of the same ages make the same kind of pottery throughout? The answer is that they did not. While it sometimes happens that similar kinds of ware are found amongst peoples widely separated in space or time, the similarity is generally superficial and far removed from absolute identity. We rely on three main factors in distinguishing different kinds of pots and sherds—the shape of the vessel, the ornament (if any) and the texture of the clay from which it is made: also upon the presence or absence of special features such as glaze or pigment and handles. The different variations of each of these factors are legion, and it is extremely improbable that the same combination should occur twice without cultural connection. The fragments of those vessels of the Early Bronze Age known as beakers are difficult to distinguish from certain fragments of North American pottery; but they *can* be distinguished, mainly by comparing the composition of the clay of which each is made. Nevertheless, while it is often possible to recognise and date potsherds at sight, it is often difficult or tedious to give a reason. This naturally annoys a scientific man if he is not an archaeologist. He objects to dogmatic opinions, unsupported by reasons. In most cases the difficulty of giving a reason for one's opinion is due, not so much to confused thinking as to the fact that one's knowledge has become subconscious or intuitive through long familiarity with one's subject; one's memories are tactile derived from the handling of thousands of other potsherds. In most cases it would be possible to give reasons, but it might take time and involve lengthy explanations. Often one bases one's opinion upon a kind of negative foundation, on the improbability of the sherds in question belonging to any other period than that to which one attributes them. They are not Roman, for instance, because they are not any of them wheel-turned, they are not of the Bronze Age because of the texture, they are probably mediaeval because of the texture which is characteristic of that period, they are almost certainly all mediaeval because some of them have the typical finger-print ornament round the edges. (The presence of this ornament on a raised rib round the top a few inches below the rim would show that they belonged to the Bronze Age, other things being equal.[1])

Let us return for a moment to the analogy between palaeontology and archaeology. The archaeologist is mainly concerned with his 'type fossils' as a means to an end, which is, the dating of sites and strata. He can give some information

[1] I have taken potsherds as examples throughout because they are the commonest and most generally useful 'type fossil' in archaeology, but, of course, the same arguments apply with equal force to other objects.

about the culture of the people from, say, potsherds, especially if they are elaborately ornamented, but it will not lead him very far. The palaeontologist, on the other hand, is very deeply concerned with the intensive study of the fossil bones and leaves and the like which he discovers, for they lead him to a knowledge of the actual structure of the living forms which clothed them. This, however, is incidental only to our present argument. For this it is of more importance to observe that the palaeontologist is now the father of the geologist, for he provides him with the means of dating rocks (whether stratified or not) to whose age there is no other clue. For instance, the discovery in America of a fossil or group of fossils characteristic of the upper chalk in Europe will enable him to equate that formation with the European system. It is to him what the Egyptian scarab was to us in the Sudan. His science, like ours, is a time-science, and is concerned with changes which have taken place on the face of the earth from the earliest times to the present day. His ultimate object, as a geologist, is, through a study of stratified deposits, to construct maps of the earth as it appeared during each successive geological period, restoring the ancient coast-line, rivers and mountain ranges.

CHAPTER VII

TIME-ASPECT AND SPACE-ASPECT

HAVING isolated his periods, the archaeologist is free to study any one of them intensively. That is to say, he sets out from the remains which he discovers to glean all that can be gleaned about the people of the period. He can learn a great deal about their ideas from their burial customs, and from the remains of structures like Stonehenge, or of shrines and sacred caves, like those in ancient Crete. He discovers much about their civilisation from their personal ornaments and charms, and if he is lucky enough to be digging in a country with a rainless climate like Egypt or Nubia he can investigate many relics of wood and cloth which elsewhere have usually perished. He can examine their knowledge of metallurgy. All this and more besides he can discover from a single site. He can find out much more by comparison with adjacent sites which—from the occurrence there of similar types, or by other means—he knows to belong to the same period. In fact, he should never if possible rely on a single site for his generalisations. There are sure to be special circumstances which make it in one way or another exceptional. Moreover it is a contravention of the logical law about generalising from particular instances. It should always be his aim to discover *the extent in space of a given culture during a given period.* How is he to set about this?

In the first place, it will be well to explain what is meant by culture. That is not at all easy. Culture may be defined as the sum of all the ideals and activities and material which characterise a group of human beings. It is to a community what character is to an individual. Obviously the archaeologist will be hard put to it to discover all this about a given community with his spade alone! But, fortunately for him, the purely intellectual activities of primitive peoples are not great or numerous, and he can discover a good deal about the probable social organisation with the help of comparisons provided by the anthropologist. It is also to his advantage that communities of kindred culture display many resemblances in their material remains as well as in their social customs. It may therefore be taken for granted that if a number of communities scattered over a given area display a uniformity in their remains, they may be classed together as forming a single homogeneous cultural group. This is true of primitive communities at the present day, and it was therefore probably true in the past. Cultural resemblances also show community of origin or close commercial relations.

The archaeologist will ascertain these common cultural areas by taking one—or, better, a group—of the 'type fossils' and plotting on a map their distribution in space. He must select typical examples, not exceptions, and he must include every recorded discovery, otherwise his results will be vitiated by a kind of artificial selection. He will also be well advised if for convenience of working he selects an area enclosed within clearly defined limits—otherwise he will be led astray by side-issues. The sea is the best frontier to choose, or, failing that, a political or provincial boundary. A clearly defined boundary of some kind is essential during the period when he is 'collecting instances'. As an example of a piece of work of this nature I will refer the reader to an article of mine which appeared in the *Geographical Journal* for 1912 (Vol. 40). I took the period known as the Early Bronze Age, and the area of the British Isles. As 'type fossils' of the period I selected the flat bronze axe (or celt) without side-flanges or stop-ridge, and the pottery vessels known as beakers (or drinking-cups). I also gave a map showing the distribution of gold lunulae, which belong to the Early Bronze Age. I compiled a list by counties of every recorded discovery of each type, and plotted on a map the exact position of each find whose site of discovery was known.

Certain very interesting results followed. In the first place, the finds fell naturally into several very distinct groups on the map. Secondly, these groups were found to be almost identical on both the flat

THE MORTLAKE BEAKER.

A typical specimen of a beaker, found in the Thames at Mortlake and now in the British Museum. Height 9·6 inches. (Scale ½.)

Facing p. 80.

TIME-ASPECT AND SPACE-ASPECT

axe and the beaker maps. This proved that the population during the Early Bronze Age was mainly concentrated over the areas where the finds were thickest, and these regions themselves were found on examination to have a very definite causal connection with geological conditions. It was seen that the groups coincided with the areas of bare chalk, such as Salisbury Plain, part of Dorsetshire, and the parts of Norfolk and Cambridgeshire forming the shores of the Fenland marshes; or areas of carboniferous limestone, like the Peak district of Derbyshire.[1] Another interesting fact which emerged was that hardly a single true beaker was found in Ireland. Of the other finds, some were grouped round the mouths of rivers where ports had probably existed, and others by their alignment suggested the course of trade-routes between groups and trade-routes across Britain, connecting Ireland with the Continent.

An attempt was also made to ascertain the areas on the Continent where beakers had been found, and a number of similar groups emerged. It was then possible to trace beakers to their source in Germany, where their centre of distribution was located. That they did not develop in these islands is proved by the fact that when first found here they are already fully developed. In Germany, on the other hand, their ancestry can be traced back through all its stages to a simple original form.

Trade connections were suggested by mapping

[1] See Note at end of Chapter.

the distribution of certain crescent-shaped ornaments of thin leaf-gold known as lunulae (or lunettes), which are found in the greatest numbers in Ireland, and of which a few specimens have been found in Great Britain and on the Continent.

Early connections with the Mediterranean were suggested by the discovery at Winterbourne Bassett in Wiltshire of a copper dagger of a well-known Mediterranean type.

The attempt was a pioneer one, and naturally its conclusions will be amplified and modified by later research.[1] But the collection of facts and the resultant maps have provided a firm foundation upon which to build. Moreover the actual results were very encouraging, and drew attention to a new aspect of prehistoric research. It was the first attempt in this country to regard a past epoch of European prehistory from a geographical point of view. The distribution of types has been mapped by Lissauer in Germany, by Pič in Bohemia and by Déchelette in France; but none of these men of science have attempted to correlate the groups with any geographical factors. This is largely due to the failure to grasp what is meant by geography. To justify this statement it will be necessary to consider what we do mean by

[1] For comments on the paper and the discussion which ensued see *Ancient Wales—Anthropological Evidences,* by Professor H. J. Fleure, University College of Wales, Aberystwyth. *Published as a separate monograph by the Honourable Society of Cymmrodorion, 1917.*

TIME-ASPECT AND SPACE-ASPECT

geography, and so we arrive at the very heart of the problem, the central idea round which this book is written.

It is that archaeology and geography are in one sense not so much sciences as *aspects*. Archaeology is *a* time-aspect (the one concerned with man); geography is *the* space-aspect.

I consider this idea to be of fundamental importance. Certain explanations, however, are necessary.

Archaeology is *a* time-science because it deals with time only in so far as man is concerned; geography, on the other hand, deals with space irrespective of the existence of man upon the earth. The geographical aspect is therefore all-embracing, and in its narrower sense where man is involved it is called ' anthropogeography ' or human geography. To get a true view of the respective functions of archaeology and geography, it will be necessary to travel over rather a wide field, and one may best begin by putting two questions and attempting to answer them. What sciences, other than archaeology, deal with time ? What are the sciences which deal with space ?

Both time and space may, for practical purposes, be taken as relative to the earth and its surface. Beyond it we come to astronomy. In passing, however, it may be observed that the methods of astronomy are curiously like those of anthropology and archaeology. The interest of astronomy centres in the solar system and the earth which forms part of it. For it is inevitable that, whether he be investigating the universe or a parish, a man's interests will be drawn first and foremost to his own home. An anthropocentric bias is latent in all his researches. It is well that it should be so, provided his vision be not distorted, for there is added to his work the touch of personal, human interest. So the astronomer is most interested to discover the origins of our own universe and of the solar system in which our earth revolves. He cannot get direct access to other universes (if such there be), but he can study the birth and childhood of other planetary systems, and so form some idea of the beginnings of our own. In the same way the anthropologist, by studying existing primitive peoples, discovers the stages through which humanity has passed in the childhood of mankind. Herein lies the importance of the study of nebulae or star-clusters, and hence came the nebular hypothesis. With the cooling of the earth and the subsequent first appearance of life, the chemist passes across the stage, and in so far as he studies the past in the light of the present (by experiment) his science is a time-science. His main interests, however, lie elsewhere. The biologist is intimately concerned with the origin of life, but he, too, works mainly by experiment. After them comes the geologist, whose science is *the* time-science *par excellence*. Assisted in his dating by the type fossils of palaeontology, he arranges the rocks of the earth's crust in the order of their formation. Like the archaeologist, he can sometimes get information from other sources than type fossils or stratification, such as intrusive rocks which break through or overflow a series of strata, or which are overlapped or covered by other strata; just as the excavator can date a barrow or other earthwork from the fact that it cuts into another which he can date by internal or other evidence. The geologist's dating becomes more difficult when he gets to later periods, and has to deal with drift formations of clays, gravels and sand that do not contain many fossils. But throughout his main problem is a time-problem —the relative age of deposits.

Again, botany, zoology, ornithology and all the host of sciences which deal with living organisms —are they not all of them part and parcel of the great science of life itself, biology ? And do not they all find their time-aspect in palaeontology, the science of the changing forms of life in the past ?

It is not, of course, maintained that either the time- or the space-aspect is the only aspect. There is a third and equally important one—the aspect of things as they are in themselves or as they behave. All branches of knowledge have this aspect, of which chemistry, physiology and psychology are typical. The archaeologist also—figuratively and actually—examines his specimens under the microscope, and describes them as they appear to him and their special significance as he sees it. The methods of this aspect are observation or experiment and description.

What, then, of the second question, of the sciences which deal with space?

All sciences deal with space, but some deal with much larger portions than others, and it is these that we have specially to consider. The astronomer claims the largest share, and he deals with three dimensions. For practical purposes we, however, may confine our attention to the two dimensions of the earth's surface. The geologist aims at arranging his strata in their proper sequence, as we have seen. But of what are these strata composed? Of deposits formed under certain conditions, either under the sea or on its shores by the sediment brought down by rivers, or by the decay of living organisms, or above water by wind-erosion acting on rocks, or by volcanic agencies from beneath the surface. His ultimate aim is to restore the relative distribution of land and sea during each of the periods represented by these strata, and to add such geographical details as he can to the land-surface and to the depths of the ocean. These aims are finely attempted and illustrated (by maps) by Haug in his admirable treatise on geology,[1] and by Suess in his truly epoch-making work, *The Face of the Earth*.[2] But no more than the bare outline of continents and oceans, with an occasional hint at glaciers and

[1] E. Haug, *Traité de géologie*, 2 vols. in 3: Paris, Armand Colin, 1907–11.

[2] English translation in 4 vols.: Oxford, Clar. Press, 1904–9. [The French translation, edited by de Margerie, is much more fully illustrated with maps, notes and diagrams than this or the German original.]

mountain-ranges, has so far been possible on the maps of the earliest geological periods. This is natural in the present state of our knowledge of the geology of large areas of the earth. A more detailed attempt at restoring ancient land-surface has been made by A. J. Jukes-Brown in his *Building of the British Isles* (3rd edition, 1911). A portion of East Anglia has been studied from this point of view by Harmer, whose results are embodied by Jukes-Brown. Harmer has restored the land-surface and estuarine conditions at the time of the formation of the Cromer Forest-bed. He has succeeded in mapping the course of a large estuary. It is not of course suggested that this process of surveying the world in past ages is an easy one or one that can be rapidly accomplished. It can only be built up gradually by regional research and the piecing together of such scraps of evidence as we have left. Nor is it forgotten that for large areas, at many epochs, hypothetical restorations alone are possible, because the evidence is either wholly wanting or hidden beneath existing oceans. It is, however, of vital importance to the study of man when we first meet with him and throughout his subsequent early career. It is as important to our knowledge of his past states as are maps of the world to-day to the soldier or the economist, or even the politician, if he could but realise it. For we need not only maps of the land and sea surfaces, we need as much detail about both as can be discovered and mapped. I will leave to abler hands the question as to how far the distribution of the vegetation of past geological epochs is capable of being shown on a map. I see no reason, however, to despair of our eventually being able to produce a tentative—perhaps somewhat diagrammatic—map of the flora of very remote periods like the carboniferous. Similarly with the fauna of past epochs. Here the geologist works in close alliance with the palaeontologist and zoologist. The zoologist points to the primitive fauna which have survived in an island-continent like Australia, and the palaeontologist infers for him the existence of a land-bridge which was severed in Jurassic times and has never since been re-formed.

NOTE (p. 81).—This method of explaining one set of distributions by means of another, both sets being dealt with cartographically, is strikingly illustrated by the following remarks of Sir David Bruce (*Daily Mail*, April 28, 1920) :—

'This led the Commission to ask the question, " Does the distribution of sleeping sickness in Uganda coincide with the distribution of any particular biting insect ? " . . . Sir Apolo Kagwa and the other head chiefs were asked to have specimens of biting flies sent in from every part of Uganda. The aid of the government officials and missionaries was also enlisted.

'In three months the Commission received some 500 collections of biting flies. As each package came in it was examined, and if it contained a tsetse fly a red disc was stuck on a large map over the locality from which the flies had been sent. If, on the other hand, no tsetse flies were found, a blue disc was stuck on.

'At the same time another map was prepared to show the distribution of sleeping sickness. That is to say, if the note accompanying the collection of flies stated that sleeping sickness was present, a red disc was placed over the locality ; if, on the contrary, no sleeping sickness was reported, a blue disc.

'After three months, on placing the two maps together they were found exactly to coincide, therefore it was taken as proved that sleeping sickness is conveyed from the sick to the healthy by the tsetse fly, *Glossina palpalis*.'

CHAPTER VIII

THE IMPORTANCE OF ENVIRONMENT

HOWEVER important (especially for educational purposes) these geological restorations of the remoter epochs may be to a proper understanding of the earth's geographical history, they do not concern us as students of man. They have been cited only as instances of method, and because they become of great importance when we get to more recent geological periods, when man begins to appear.

A study of its environment is essential to a proper understanding of any organism. Though this fact is now generally recognised, its corollary is not—namely, that the study of the environment of a *group* of organisms is equally necessary to a proper understanding of the group ; and when we get to groups the environment at .once becomes geographical. I will take three instances to illustrate this.

We know that man existed in Europe while great parts of the continent were covered by an ice-sheet. We are gradually getting to be able to equate the successive phases of glaciation with successive culture-periods. As soon as this equation is complete — nay, when we have certainly equated a single human period with a geological one—it will be of the utmost importance to compare the relations between the area occupied by man, on the one hand, and the extent of the ice-sheet and of the dry land-surface on the other. There will also be other features which we shall want to know more about—the probable course of rivers, the distribution of marginal lakes, vegetation, the areas of high and low elevation and the climatic conditions. We shall also want to know how far the different geographical conditions then obtaining tended to make habitable large desert areas like the Sahara. Regarding the problem from the time-aspect, we shall be able to trace the gradual movement of man northwards on the heels of the retreating ice-sheet, the probable spur to progress and increase in numbers produced in the old areas by a more favourable environment, and the late survival of the old ousted cultures in their less favourable northern surroundings.

We see, then, what an important factor is environment. I said above that the aims of archaeology were to discover by every means in our power all that can be discovered about man in past ages. It will now, I hope, be clear to the reader (and more so if he have patience to read the next few chapters) that to know everything possible about the men of a given epoch it is necessary also to study their environment. This must first be restored and portrayed in the form of maps by the specialists concerned, chiefly the geologist, botanist, zoologist and climatologist. In the instance quoted in Chapter I. the most influential factor in the environment was forests. To prove the hypothesis outlined we need to know the distribution of forests during each successive stage, and we need to know it in some detail. Further, we need proofs that at a certain point of time the forests began to disappear, thus compelling man (or his arboreal ancestor) to take to a life on the ground.

It is of the utmost importance to British archaeologists to know at what archaeological period the straits of Dover came into existence and Britain became an island. The effects of this insulation are too obvious to need enumeration. If the cutting of the straits took place before the art of navigation was discovered, the effects would of course be very great indeed.

As a last instance of the importance of environment I will take a later period, the neolithic. It is well known that in certain parts of England stone (generally flint) arrowheads are very commonly found, whereas in others they are extremely rare. So far as I know no attempt has ever been made to show this distribution geographically, or to correlate it with any geographical factor. But such correlation will probably explain the discontinuity of the distribution.

Take the Haslemere district of Surrey, the neighbourhood of the Devil's Punch-bowl. In the Haslemere museum are a great number of flint arrowheads all found within this small region. Now at the present day most of the area where they occur consists of open commons, principally covered with heather and bracken. It has remained waste land because the soil (greensand) is barren, and unsuitable either for pasturage or for agriculture. Here we have a region which even now is unsuitable for agriculture — much more must it have been so in the past when more fertile soils were still available. Such an area would, however, be admirably adapted to the requirements of a hunting community, for it would abound in deer and other game, while the close proximity of forests on the Wealden Clay would provide an occasional wild pig. The hunter's chief weapon was the bow and arrow; and arrowheads naturally got lost in large numbers. Hence we may conclude that their abundance in this neighbourhood is ultimately due to the barrenness of the soil, and the consequent fauna and flora which it produced; and also to the plentiful supply of good flint available in the chalk of the Wealden escarpment close at hand.

In striking contrast with the abundance of arrowheads round Haslemere is their extreme scarcity over the adjacent uplands of the Basingstoke district. Here the prevalent types of flint implement are scrapers and the chipped or ground flint

THE IMPORTANCE OF ENVIRONMENT 93

axe. It is probable that the Hampshire axes, some of which are of very rough workmanship, were mounted like adzes or even as hoes, and were used for breaking up the soil. Over these Hampshire uplands the soil is chalk, sometimes covered with a capping of clay with flints. It would have been well adapted to primitive agriculture.

Obviously, before any extensive correlations of this kind can be established, we must have maps showing the distribution of different types of vegetation at different periods. More than anything else, we need as a basis a vegetation-map of the British Isles at, say, the neolithic period before any appreciable attempt had been made at cutting down and clearing forests. But the British Isles present only a single example of a need which is world-wide. There is required [1] a series of maps showing the distribution of land and sea during all past geological and later epochs, getting more and more detailed and larger in scale as we approach later and better known periods. We want an Atlas of Geographical Environment,—the face of the earth as it appeared in successive epochs. (We really need a series of globes, especially for the earlier stages, and for showing the mechanism of folding; for it is impossible fully to appreciate on a flat surface the exact processes involved and the functions of large resistant 'massifs'.) There

[1] I speak as an amateur student of geology and of this aspect of it in particular. It will, of course, be for professional geologists to produce such maps for all periods except the present, and for the botanists, etc., to embellish them.

will be agreement as to scales, which should be on a uniform system of, say, three throughout; and there must also be a standard system of conventional signs, colouring, etc. We might perhaps include in such an Atlas an appendix of certain notable attempts at regional restoration. Such an attempt and the three scales adopted could be relative to three main areas: (1) the whole surface of the earth; (2) the old world, especially Europe; (3) Western Europe, especially the British Isles.[1]

Such an orientation, though not strictly logical, is desirable to secure the best results. We can safely leave it to our friends in West and East to produce an Atlas with an Atlantic and Pacific orientation.

Of course our Atlas would be only a preliminary step towards the ideal. It would not be intended to be final, but it would be as perfect as the present state of our knowledge allowed. Later editions would be published, improved in the light of criticisms of the first, and embodying the results of subsequent research. The publication of such an Atlas of Geographical Environment would give a tremendous impetus to all investigations conducted on the lines which are advocated in this book.

[1] I suggest the scales of 1/10,000,000, 1/1,000,000 and 1/250,000.

CHAPTER IX

ARCHAEOLOGY AND OTHER BRANCHES OF SCIENCE

WE are now in a position to realise a little more clearly which are the sciences that deal with space.

Pre-eminent amongst them is geology, for it deals ultimately with pure space, as also with pure time. From it can be seen most clearly what is meant by the time- and space-aspect of a science. In the last resort geology is concerned with little else but the lapse of time over the whole surface of the earth, for the deepest sedimentary rock was once the topmost film of all.

But there are other sciences no less concerned with space. When once the geologist has restored the ancient land-surface, it is for the student of life in all its forms to people it with plants and animals — and this at every period, each on a separate map. The mineralogist, in particular, will help the archaeologist by approaching the study of metals more geographically than hitherto, by mapping the distribution of such metals as are most useful to man. As their distribution has hardly altered since man appeared—and then only by man's own agency, through the exhaustion of deposits — his task is an easy one. Hitherto the geographer has had to map these distributions, but obviously he can only take the results of specialists, and he is really doing their work for them. If the importance (shown in the last chapter) of studying an organism, or group of organisms, in relation to its environment were fully realised, this would not be so. We archaeologists in particular—as students of humanity—need the help of other sciences, but we ought not to be obliged to do their work. It lies with us, however, to point out to them that by studying the geographical aspect of their sciences not only will they be helping us archaeologists enormously, but they will be working on truly scientific lines, and incidentally they will be adding a really human interest to their work.

For there is no such thing as pure geography. There is instead a geographical aspect of many sciences. As has been pointed out by Colonel Sir Charles Close (in his Presidential Address to Section E of the British Association at Portsmouth in 1911), the geographer can only take the results of other sciences and map them. If education were conducted on more broadly scientific lines— in other words, if it were more geographical—the importance of the geographical aspect of their own branch of science would become apparent; and our men of science would produce maps themselves, and much more satisfactory ones than the amateur geographer can ever hope to achieve. At present the maps that are made fail in their purpose, because they are produced either by amateurs of one subject or by scientific specialists who have no notion of map-making. If instruction in elementary map-drawing were part of a liberal education, the charge of narrow interests would be largely removed from scientific specialists. They would be led to take an intelligent interest in the study of man, and might even in their spare time conduct reprisals upon the geographer and the archaeologist for past raids into their territory —reprisals which both, I think, would welcome! For it is up to all those who attack geography as a science to justify their attacks by doing the work which the geographer has now to do for them, and which he naturally does imperfectly.

Let me now revert to my paper on the Early Bronze Age, discussed above. I take this piece of work as a model, because it was written with that object, and because, till it was written, nothing had been published which dealt in quite the same geographical way with a problem of prehistoric archaeology. That essay was incomplete in many respects. For instance, the environment was inadequately treated; a vegetation map should have been shown. But none was available for the period in question, and I had not the time to compile even a rough outline one, nor the necessary equipment of botanical knowledge to produce a satisfactory map even if I had had the time. It is the business of the botanist to map the vegetation of past periods. The ordinary geographer cannot be expected to do so.[1] Yet our study of the social and economic conditions of man in the Bronze Age, and in all others down to and including the present, is hampered by lack of just this knowledge shown adequately in map-form. We need to know the relative areas covered by forest, grass-land and marsh in order, firstly, to determine the state of culture of the inhabitants of a region — were they in a hunting, pastoral or agricultural stage?[2] Secondly, to know, at any rate approximately, the relative density of population and the different regions in which it was concentrated. We need also to discover the blank spaces. Then we shall find out what barriers isolated different areas, hindering or preventing intercourse. A dense forest with under-growth will prove a more effective isolating barrier than one where the trees grow further apart, and where savannah or park-like conditions prevail.[3] The importance of these

[1] It is of course possible that a few exceptionally gifted persons may succeed in combining in themselves the specialised knowledge of many sciences. But in the present state of secondary education it would be absurd to expect the average scientific student to be botanist, zoologist, climatologist, geologist, mineralogist, economist and more besides—all at once! It is quite certain that no living ' geographer ' is such an ' admirable Crichton '. My point here is that he should not attempt it, but should rather be able to depend, for the geographical aspect, on the specialists concerned.

[2] In determining a problem like this, archaeological evidence is often meaningless unless taken in conjunction with the contemporary environment. Witness the Haslemere arrowheads referred to above in Chapter IV.

[3] As once probably in Herefordshire.

factors is being slowly realised in the study of continents like Africa, inhabited still, for the most part, by primitive peoples. It is beginning to be realised in the study of history, though but slowly in this country. But even so, only a few attempts have been made to map the conditions adequately, and thus to make an appeal to the eye. We need maps — maps of everything, in every text-book (whatever its subject) and in every monograph and scientific paper—not mere diagrams inserted in the text and only two or three inches in size, but real, large-scale maps with colours.

We archaeologists must make friends with the mineralogists and induce them to study and to map for us the distribution of certain metals which were of primary importance in prehistoric times. It is a commonplace to connect the distribution of population with that of coal at the present day. The exact coincidence of the areas of densest population with regions where coal is found is obvious on comparing a geological map with a map showing the density of population (see Bartholomew's *Economic Atlas*). The two maps are complementary : the one explains the other. (In prehistoric times this agreement is not found as regards *density* of population, but the economic tie is just as close and binding in other ways.) To study the present distribution of population (which is the economist's business) without reference to the geological map is ridiculous. There is a geographical aspect of economic science as of other sciences. The archaeologist, in so far as he is studying a past aspect of economic science, is an economist. 'Social archaeology' is the social and economic aspect of society in successive ages of the past. Put in another way, economic science is the equivalent at the present day of social archaeology. That is what I mean by calling archaeology an aspect. It is the time-aspect of economics and other sciences. But the road to the economic study of problems of the past can only be prepared by certain preliminary work which the archaeologist is specially trained to carry out —by excavation and by the interpretation of discoveries, by the classification of types in order of development, and by the subsequent mapping of their distribution.

But to return. There is an opening for a mineralogist who will plot on a map for us the distribution of certain metals, such as gold, copper, tin, lead and antimony, differentiated according as they occur pure in their native state, in ore or in stream deposits. An attempt was made to construct some maps of this kind to illustrate my Early Bronze Age paper. The distribution of gold, copper and tin was shown on a map of the British Isles. In passing, it should be noted that it is as important in a map of this kind to show graphically the areas where the metals in question are *not* found in a natural state as it is to show those where they do occur. The blank spaces are evidence of a negative kind often representing

ARCHAEOLOGY, ETC.

a great deal of research. These blank areas should not be clipped off the edges of the map.[1] For instance, it is of the utmost importance to show geographically the fact that gold, copper and tin are not found naturally in any part of southern or eastern England; for over just this region prehistoric objects made from these metals are very abundant. It follows that they—or the raw metal of which they were made—must have been introduced into these regions by trade.

Commercial relations between communities are of the utmost importance to a study of the past, as of the present, and it is the business of the archaeologist, firstly, to establish the existence of such relations, and, secondly, to determine their exact nature and the routes followed. When the sources of the raw material have been carefully mapped by the scientist concerned, the archaeologist will have a firm foundation to build upon.[2]

As an extreme instance of the value of the discovery of objects foreign to the locality in throwing light on trade, and also of the dependence of the archaeologist upon the geographical aspect of other sciences, may be taken the discovery

---

[1] The same applies to maps of archaeological distributions. Areas which have been worked over by the student and found blank should always be shown.

[2] It should be observed that, until mineralogists, botanists and the rest produce such maps, the archaeologist is perfectly justified in producing his own. Their very inadequacy, incompleteness and, it may very likely be, inaccuracy, should prove an incentive to the specialist to correct them by producing better ones himself. It is the author's intention to act thus himself, if he is enabled to do so.

of the lip of a cowry-shell (*Cypraea minor*) in an Early Iron Age settlement on the site of Hurstbourne Station (L. & S.W.R. main line) in Hampshire. The age of the settlement was proved by the character of the potsherds and by the finding of a gold coin of a well-known type. The present distribution of such shells is confined to the Red Sea littoral. The question of the species and its present distribution was dealt with by Mr. J. R. le B. Tomlin.[1] We have to explain how the shell in question (which was probably worn as an amulet) travelled in prehistoric times from the Red Sea to Hampshire. The instance is, as I have said, an extreme one, but it illustrates my point. Another similar problem during the same period is presented by the existence of fragments of red coral in certain Early Iron Age cemeteries in Yorkshire and elsewhere. The coral in question has not, so far as I am aware, been studied and reported on by a specialist, and no map has been made of its distribution. Hence, though we know it must probably have come from the Mediterranean, we are still in the dark as to the exact locality from which it was derived.

Another substance whose distribution requires mapping is amber. Large numbers of beads and other objects of amber are found in prehistoric sites of all ages. It has been assumed that it was derived from the shores of the Baltic, but it occurs

[1] Paper read at a Meeting of the Linnaean Society, June 14, 1911.

naturally on the eastern shores of Britain, as well as on those of the Mediterranean and Black Sea. We need some one who will undertake to analyse and classify the different varieties known, refer them to their respective origins, and map the distribution of each kind. But, first of all, the amber should be studied in its natural state, and specimens should be procured from each region for analysis. When the different natural varieties have been determined and their distribution mapped, the archaeologist can proceed to map the distribution of each kind as he finds it, made into beads and other objects.

The same methods may be applied to the distribution of flint. This mineral occurs naturally either in veins in the chalk or in gravel deposits (derived ultimately, of course, from the chalk).

Now in certain regions, like Wales and Cornwall, flint occurs as a part of the constituents of ancient and modern sea-beaches, though no chalk occurs now in either district. Prehistoric man had a very sharp eye for flint, and he used these deposits very freely. I have suggested the importance of mapping these flint deposits in a paper contributed to *Archaeologia Cambrensis* (July 1917). The object of such a flint survey in Wales and Cornwall (for what I said in it applies equally to Cornwall) is to ascertain what spots along the coast and elsewhere would have had an additional attraction for prehistoric man. The coast should be examined, and specimens of the flint pebbles found should be collected in bags, each with a pencil note *written on the spot* giving details of exact site, percentage of flints in whole deposit, maximum size and colour of flint pebbles, and many other points which suggest themselves as of importance. Similar collections should be made of worked fragments of flakes, efforts being made to secure pieces with part of the original outer core adhering. When such a survey is complete we shall be able to compare any flint implements found, say, in excavations of a cave or inland site, with our specimens in bags (now stored in a museum for reference). We shall be able to say with some degree of certainty whether the implement in question was made from local flint pebbles and, if so, from what locality they came. We shall also be able to say definitely that certain finer and larger implements, like axes, could not have been made from flint pebbles, because none are found big enough, and because the quality of the axe is such that it appears to have been made from a block quarried directly from the chalk. The tracing of these axes to their source is a fascinating problem which awaits solution. I will merely suggest in passing that the inquiry should proceed along certain obvious lines: (1) The mapping of all recorded finds of flint implements and factories (especially where there is no local flint available as a source of supply). (2) The critical and analytical examination of the flint of which the implements are made. (3) The reference of the flint to its origin by a comparison of

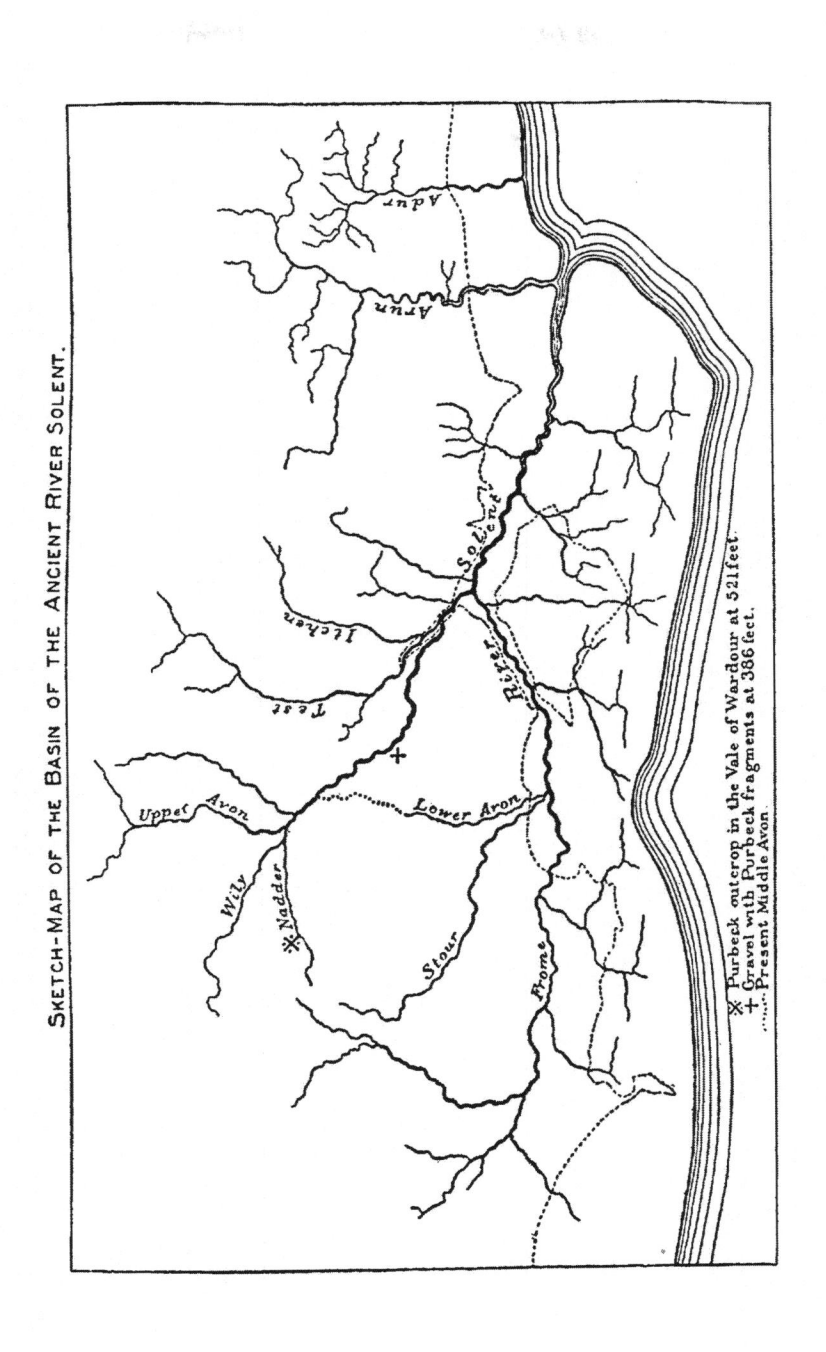

Sketch-Map of the Basin of the Ancient River Solent.

the material with vein-flint of different qualities, helped by the type to which the implement itself belongs.

The result of all these investigations will be a clearer knowledge of economic and commercial conditions in prehistoric times. That is their main object.

The methods by which the archaeologist discovers trade-routes by tracing raw materials like amber or gold to their natural source is closely paralleled in geology. Let me give an instance. Certain high-level gravels near Alderbury in Wiltshire contain a small percentage of stones which are not flint but are derived from oolitic formations. Now the nearest outcrop of oolitic rocks occurs in the valley of the Nadder, and the obvious and correct conclusion is that these stones were brought down by a river which flowed from the region where the oolitic rocks outcrop. We are thus able to restore the course of this ancient river, just as we restore the course of a prehistoric trade-route. (See map.)

Similarly we study the movements of glaciers through the distribution of erratic blocks.

CHAPTER X

THE MAIN FACTORS IN MAN'S ENVIRONMENT

IN the preceding chapter I took certain sciences which deal with space, and showed how dependent the archaeologist is upon their results, which he desires to be portrayed graphically by means of maps.[1] I selected the botanist and mineralogist, and it was seen that both could throw light on the general cultural conditions of a given period, and that the mineralogist in particular could help greatly in the matter of prehistoric trade. I now propose to consider the results to be obtained

---

[1] The publication of these results should take the form of a monograph in a cardboard cover, with a series of maps in a pocket at the end of the book or entirely detached. The letterpress should consist of a full inventory or schedule with details (bibliographical and descriptive) such as cannot conveniently be shown on the maps. There should also be a short descriptive text, setting forth the problem which it is proposed to solve, describing the distributions shown on the maps and the conclusions to be drawn from them, and any pet theories of the author. The maps and the inventories are the main thing. Hitherto the map (if any) has been regarded as illustrating the article or monograph it accompanies. This reverses the logical sequence. It is as if the Ordnance Survey published their field-books and diaries in full, and relegated the map itself to a position of minor importance.

Maps are a fresh notation, more comprehensive than pictures, more succinct than language, and international.

from co-operation between the archaeologist, the botanist and the zoologist; and to show how the archaeologist can improve his own work and widen his interest by studying his results from the standpoint of social archaeology.

It has been shown above that a reconstruction of the environment is essential to a study of prehistoric man. The most important factors in this environment are position, climate, soil, vegetation and animals other than man. Both vegetation and animals may be divided into two classes, wild and domesticated (or cultivated). The whole forms a complex, none of whose compound parts should be studied separately: further, the component parts are themselves a complex of individual factors or organisms. Over any given area at the present day, where natural vegetation flourishes undisturbed, the sum total of the plant-life represents that particular association of plants which has survived in the struggle for existence by being best adapted to its environment. That environment in the case of plant-life is composed of climate, soil and position;[1] and it varies according to each variation in these component factors of the environment. For instance, a clay soil will produce entirely different plant associations in a dry and a wet climate; and the most favourable soil is barren where there is no rainfall at all. Similarly, position on a wind-swept

[1] Vertical, whether at high or low altitudes: or horizontal, whether near the sea or in marshes, etc.

shore will greatly affect plant-life, and trees in particular.

Fortunately, however, the archaeologist is not greatly concerned with plant associations in the past except in so far as they affect man; and this they do in several ways. Take the distribution of forests, for instance, or of scrub, heather moors and pasture lands. How is it possible to restore their distribution in past ages? There are several ways. The only absolute proof of the existence of a given tree or plant at a given place and time is from direct archaeological evidence—the finding of its remains or seed on an ancient site. Such discoveries have been made in a Roman well at Silchester, but I do not know of any attempt by plant oecologists to make use of their evidence in restoring the vegetation of the Silchester district in Roman times. Certainly no oecological map has been compiled, and that, after all, is the main thing. The date of the introduction of certain trees, elm and pine in particular, is of the utmost importance. A separate monograph on each of these trees, written by a botanist from the standpoint of human geography, would be invaluable. But he *must* realise what is wanted, and that what is important to him as a botanist may be negligible as a factor in human environment, and vice versa. A botanist with the orientation, so to speak, of anthropogeography could surely discover quite a lot that would be welcomed by the student of prehistoric man. He, too, is alone capable of appreciating the significance of facts and associations which are but dry lists of names to the archaeologist. The results might in many cases be purely negative, but even negative results are better than none at all; for they show us where we stand and what we need to discover, and thus provide a starting-point and stimulus for future investigations. For archaeological excavators are beginning to realise the importance of recording their minor discoveries, and that every fact gleaned from the past has a value and meaning of its own, which is enhanced by its age, especially if that age can be stated in definite terms. On the principle of working from the known to the unknown, a start might be made by extending the admirable survey of plant associations begun by Mr. C. E. Moss. It will then, at any rate, be easier to compile a map (on a scale of, say, ten miles to the inch) showing the vegetation of the British Isles during the neolithic period, before any extensive areas were cleared or brought under cultivation. But the surveyor should have one eye on the past throughout, and should bear in mind the needs of the archaeologist in forming his groups of plant association. For the first problem of the archaeological botanist is to restore the primitive vegetation and then to trace the gradual extension of forest-clearing and cultivation. During the later periods, especially the mediaeval, the evidence becomes increasingly technical, and it might well be left for an intelligent archaeologist

VIEW ON WOODCOTT DOWN, HANTS.

Showing lynchets and junipers.

Facing p. 111.

NATURAL VEGETATION ON LITCHFIELD DOWN, HANTS.

Facing p. 111.

MAN'S ENVIRONMENT 111

with botanical leanings. But, first, it is essential to provide him with a solid basis by compiling a map of the primitive neolithic vegetation. Throughout I plead for a more human orientation of the sciences not directly concerned with man.

One of the best ways of restoring primitive vegetation is to take the different patches which still survive as islands in the rising sea of cultivation, and to work outwards from them. In many places on the chalk downs of Wessex such ' islands ' still remain unsubmerged. Where the chalk is bare of clay the usual growth is fine, close turf, with a thin scrub of juniper.[1] Elsewhere, where the chalk is covered with a thin layer of clay-with-flints, the turf gives place to a rank grass, with gorse or bracken and heather, and even small trees such as hawthorn and stunted oaks. The whole of the New Forest, outside the enclosures, is true virgin forest and heath, which has never been under plough. By taking such patches of natural scenery and carefully examining the underlying soil in each case, it is possible to restore the primitive vegetation with moderate accuracy. But some knowledge of plants, trees and shrubs, and the soils they prefer is essential, even if it be acquired only by dint of untrained observation. A more

[1] Quarley Hill in Hampshire is a good example. It can be seen from the L. & S.W.R. main line to Salisbury, between that place and Andover, near Grately, on the north side of the line. Other patches are Savernake Forest, the New Forest, and in the midlands Cannock Chase and Charnwood Forest. The moorlands of Devon, Cornwall, Yorkshire and elsewhere are of course similar patches on a larger scale.

thorough botanical training is however desirable, and, equipped with this and a geological ' drift map ', it should be fairly easy to restore the primitive vegetation over a homogeneous area like Wessex or Wales, especially if the evidence of archaeological excavations be taken into consideration.

It is obvious that to produce a primitive vegetation map for a large area like the British Isles, we must first make a map of the different soils that are found there. Such maps already exist for certain regions, in the drift-maps published by the Geological Survey on a scale of one mile to the inch.[1] There are still, however, some regrettable lacunae, notably the Marlborough Sheet (No. 285), which is badly needed to complete the Wessex area. Moreover the mapping of drifts is not quite the same thing as the mapping of soils. The one is a geological business pure and simple, and what is unimportant from a geological point of view may often be of vital importance to the plant-oecologist. The work, too, done by the geological surveyors, good though it is in the main, was done by men not intimately acquainted with the different localities. Hence there are many shortcomings which a close study by a resident would rectify. The problem is well adapted for regional investigation, for it requires that intimate personal familiarity which can only be acquired by long years of observa-

[1] The original survey of the geological drift-maps was made and plotted on the six-inch O.S. maps, and these manuscript copies can be consulted free of charge on application at the Geological Museum, Jermyn Street, London.

tion. Only a resident, and a good walker at that, can get to know a region well enough to know where to find good exposures in banks and chalk- or clay-pits, quarries, sunken roads and the like. A soil survey made in the field on the six-inch O.S. maps is one of the first pieces of work that should be undertaken by any scheme of Regional Survey. Meanwhile we must get along as best we can and produce our own vegetation maps, in the hope that their very inadequacy will stimulate some plant oecologist into action : and that he in turn will infect a geologist with his enthusiasm.

It has been remarked above that different soils under different climatic conditions produce totally different plant associations. In extreme cases this is obvious. In a wet climate a clay soil produces forest, but in a dry one the clay becomes arid desert. Corresponding variations will be made by variations in the climate. It is therefore necessary to ascertain whether any alterations in climate (especially rainfall) can be observed in past epochs. This is not easy, and the evidence is usually derived from the character of the vegetation, particularly during the palaeolithic period. We must therefore beware of arguing in a circle. However, man is an adaptable creature, and from a human standpoint climate itself is not so directly important as the resulting vegetation. Great variations in climate, of course, are important, for they affect his whole manner of living, but minor ones, especially in these islands, are comparatively negligible in their influence upon the environment. They become proportionately greater in importance as we reach regions of diminished rainfall, until finally when we reach the steppe-lands of Central Asia and the pasture-lands of Central and Southern Europe they become the dominant factor in the migrations of people. That is because, while in Western Europe the rainfall is almost always sufficient and more than sufficient to maintain life, elsewhere it is barely adequate, and a continued annual deficiency may be just enough to upset the equilibrium. It may result in the desiccation of large areas of pasture-land which become semi-desert, or in a shrinking of rivers and a consequent reduction of the areas where life (human and vegetable) is possible.[1]

The evidence for such changes of climate is manifold. It is to be found in old lake-levels (as round the Caspian), in abandoned irrigation works in now waterless regions, in dried-up wells,[2] and in the deposits of gravel or peat in valleys and on moorlands. Unlike the survey of soils the study of ancient climates is not adapted for regional study, except in so far as a single line of evidence is pursued and examined analytically. Even so,

[1] Such, for instance, is what has happened in the Tarim Basin, where life is made possible only by irrigation, and where a shrinking of rivers towards their sources, and a total drying-up of some, have produced just these effects. See the writings of Sir Aurel Stein and Ellsworth Huntington.

[2] Such as that excavated by Lieut.-General Pitt-Rivers in Cranborne Chase, where a Roman bucket was found on the dry bottom, proving a subsequent lowering of the water-level.

it is usually resolved into a problem which demands excavation for its solution. The factors of which climate is made up — rainfall, temperature and winds — act over too large an area at a time, for any local aspects to be mapped. The investigations will best be conducted by synthetical methods — by co-ordinating a number of scattered facts all bearing on the same problem. We need climatic maps of the world in successive periods of the past, compiled from contemporary scraps of evidence, before we can profitably consider the past climate of the smaller regions. Our methods are precisely analogous to those of the weather experts, whose maps in the *Times* are a daily joy. By plotting the simultaneously recorded observations of pressure, rainfall and wind-direction, a map of the weather conditions at a given moment during the past twenty-four hours is obtained, from which the weather of the ensuing twenty-four hours is forecasted. In our islands, where the weather (which is ' daily climate ') comes generally from the west, the problem is peculiarly difficult. For there are at present few opportunities of obtaining regular information (even by wireless) over the Atlantic. It is therefore necessary to complete the curves of pressure by inference. The same difficulties meet us in the past in the gaps in our evidence, and they may be surmounted in an analogous manner. The problem is one of the most difficult we have to face, but there is no reason to despair of an ultimate solution if we tackle it in the right way.

We have now considered three out of the five factors in environment—soil, climate and vegetation—and we are left with two—animals other than man, and position. How are we going to restore the distribution of the animals which primitive man struggled against and lived upon? The problem is a comparatively easy one. Wherever we find remains of prehistoric man, there (in almost every case) we find the remains of his food. Animal bones are amongst the commonest finds which are brought to light by excavation, so much so as to become embarrassing to the excavator. Often he feels inclined to return them unrecorded to the place of their discovery! But he ought not to do so until they have been examined and reported on by an expert anatomist. For we intend to find geographical work for our comparative anatomist in mapping the distribution of the animals whose remains are discovered.[1] The student of animal anatomy, the zoologist, has his problems of past distribution like all other men of science, and we do not intend to let him off any more lightly than them; for animals are closely concerned with prehistoric man as part of his environment.

A great deal of interest is added to reports of archaeological excavations when an attempt is made to interpret the animal remains found,

[1] I am referring particularly to wild species; domesticated ones will be dealt with later.
The mapping referred to will, of course, be synthetical, combining the results of all available recorded excavations and discoveries.

and to distinguish between wild and domesticated species. It gives life to the dry bones of ox, horse, sheep, pig and dog when inferences are made as to their importance to the men of the period in question. Such inferences are always more valuable if made by the excavator himself. There is a danger that archaeologists will bury their results in lists, leaving them there to be resurrected a second time by the real enthusiast. This tendency is still prevalent at the present time. It would be a good thing if the excavator were free with his own opinions, for he has during his digging subconsciously absorbed a number of valuable impressions which must help to form and guide his judgement. It is, for instance, difficult to obtain in any other way that impression of *quantity*, and of the common or rare occurrence of objects, which is often so instructive. He should, of course, check his impressions whenever possible, but he should set them on record with any qualifications that may be necessary. (This applies not only to inferences relating to animal bones but to the whole of his work.)

Lastly, we come to position. By this I mean position relative to the earth's surface and to the forces of nature. In practice this resolves itself into a question of climate. There is another kind of position, relative to human activities, of which I shall speak later. For the moment we are concerned with position as latitude and longitude and altitude. Differences in the two former, that is differences of horizontal position, lead to differences in climate, through the variations in the power of the sun's rays acting in conjunction with terrestrial elements in high and low latitudes; differences in altitude, that is in vertical position, lead to contrasts of heat and cold due to the rarefication of the upper air. They are thus both climatic factors. There are, of course, some direct influences, such as the dark pigment of the negro (if it be really due to the sun). Long residence at great altitudes is said to enlarge the lungs and strengthen the leg-muscles, while life in the plains produces the opposite effect. Contrast, for instance, the inhabitants of the Andean plateaus with those of the Sudan. These are, however, influences of minor importance. The chief influences are those of the sea, and these rapidly become involved in others of a human origin when navigation and trade supervene. Position near the sea affects the lives of men in many ways. Firstly, it tends to make them depend upon gathering shell-fish for their living, like the shell-mound people of Denmark. The sea attracts to its margin the inhabitants of every country, even those who might otherwise prefer to live inland, because it provides an easy living for the lazy. The imagination readily conjures up a vision of the earliest inhabitants of such coastal regions as sturdy and adventurous fisherfolk: but the truth is that, so far as the evidence of shell-mounds goes, many of them at any rate confined their adventures to the shore, between high and low water-mark. They were, in fact, merely beach-combers.

In the main, position is important in its relation to complex human factors, and it will be dealt with later under that heading.

CHAPTER XI

MAN'S INFLUENCE UPON HIS ENVIRONMENT

THE history of civilisation is the history of the gradual reversal of man's place in nature; it sees the wane of the influence of environment on man, and the growth of his control over that environment. With the appearance of man we at once see the beginnings of this process. For ages man was as the beasts that perish; with them he was at the mercy of nature. Slowly but surely he has turned the tables upon her. That hand whose grasp had been developed among the branches he presently turned to more subtle uses on the ground, sharpening sticks into spears and chipping stones into scrapers and hand-axes. Having once laid his hand upon nature, he has held her through all her protean changes in an ever-tightening grip. But though held, she is always there, ready to turn and rend him if the grip be relaxed but for a moment.

It may seem at first sight that this turning of the tables would involve the decay of geographical influences. The process is not one of decay but of diffusion. So long as man has his being upon this planet, so long will he be to some extent subject to the natural forces by which it is regulated. He can best adapt his environment to his own needs by studying these forces, and by so doing he will learn how to curb some and release others—to dam the river and swell its flood. As civilisation spreads over the globe, the direct influence of geographical environment becomes modified, because artificial means are found to overcome the geographic factor of space, which, stated in terms of human geography, is—distance between communities. Man may also impose artificial restrictions such as tariffs, but ultimately he is dependent on the source of raw material. He may even succeed some day in creating synthetically a large number of natural products, but he can only do so by studying their composition and structure, and by bringing together artificially the elements of which they are composed. He will thus enormously increase the raw material at his disposal, but he will still be dependent for supplies of it upon some source or other on this planet.

We can trace this process of diffusion at work in prehistoric times most clearly of all. The earliest vessels were probably made of gourd-shells, natural hollow stones, or woven grass baskets lined with clay. The last, when brought near a fire, may have suggested the use of the clay lining without its supporting basket framework, through the hardening of the clay by the heat of the fire. When once this discovery was made and adopted the community was freed at once from its dependence on the supply of grass or reeds for weaving the baskets. But it was still dependent as before on a source from which clay could be obtained. In the same way man was at first dependent upon copper and tin for fashioning his principal weapons of defence. The natural supplies of these metals are not abundant, and, especially in the case of tin, are restricted to a few widely separated localities. When once he found that harder and better implements could be made of iron (whose ores are far more common) he was freed from yet another bond of environment, to be bound in turn by another but lighter one.

The same process of liberation is going on to-day. We have witnessed within the last century man's emancipation from dependence upon animal transport by his discovery of how to use the latent forces of coal and oil. He uses water either as steam (generated by coal or oil) to drive engines, or (combined with gravity) as power to generate electricity. But he is dependent upon natural sources for coal and oil, and upon the physical configuration of the earth, causing waterfalls, for his electric power-stations.

The process is all along a liberating process, because it destroys the binding monopoly of a single or restricted source of supply, or of the inhabitants of a peculiarly favoured region. As students of man we are concerned with each stage

INFLUENCE UPON ENVIRONMENT

in this liberation : as enlightened students we are particularly interested in its geographic aspects.

Of all the plants which man has succeeded in cultivating, wheat is by far the most important. Yet its origin is still uncertain.[1] The places where it grows in a wild state appear to be known, but I know of no standard modern archaeological work wherein the question is fully discussed. A monograph is much needed, tracing its origin and dispersal along certain lines, with botanical notes on the different varieties and their pedigree. The botanist who collects material for such a monograph will draw largely upon the results of excavations in Egypt, Mesopotamia, and in the Swiss and other lake-villages. The importance of corn in studying past cultures is fundamental. The whole system by which primitive peoples are classified culturally depends upon it—as the word ' culture ' itself implies. Corn is the chief product of agriculture, and when he enters upon the agricultural stage, primitive man has made one of the greatest possible advances from savagery. For he ceases then to rely for a living upon the caprices of nature, whether in the supply of game or the uncertain harvest of wild fruit, berries and shellfish.

In the Western Hemisphere the same problems arise, but maize is the only cereal involved. In

[1] J. Brunhes, *La Géographie humaine*, 2nd ed., Paris, 1912, p. 257. See also for the whole subject A. de Candolle, *L'Origine des plantes cultivées*, 2nd ed., Paris, 1896.

Australia corn was unknown before the arrival of the white man.

Other plants upon which monographs are needed are those which are specially characteristic of the Mediterranean region, such as the olive, vine, fig, palm and orange. An admirable monograph on the olive has been written by Theobald Fischer.[1] It is, however, written rather from the standpoint of modern economics than of archaeology, with which aspect it does not deal. This, however, is no doubt largely due to the great advances in our knowledge of Mediterranean prehistorics since 1904.

The history of the vine is important, especially in early Aegean history. An interesting if comparatively unimportant monograph might also be written on its mediaeval culture in England by monasteries.

Before the discovery of the sugar-cane and of the means of extracting sugar from beetroot, honey was of far more importance than it is to-day. Hence the archaeologist and historian should keep an eye open for indications of bee-keeping and the collection of wild honey. The frequent occurrence of 'honeyways' in Anglo-Saxon Charters needs explanation. Honey was of course used in the brewing of mead, the Anglo-Saxon equivalent of beer.

I do not mean to imply that these plants

---

[1] 'Der Ölbaum, seine geographische Verbreitung, seine wirtschaftliche und kulturhistorische Bedeutung', *Petermann's Mitteilungen*, Erganzungsheft No. 147. Gotha, 1904, 87 pp. and one map 1/10,000,000.

INFLUENCE UPON ENVIRONMENT

(described above and below) are all equally capable of geographic treatment. I only wish to draw the attention of archaeologists, and especially excavators, to certain factors which are often overlooked, but which occupied a very important place in the economy of primitive and ancient communities. Nothing which helps to throw light on the manner of living—in a single word, the culture—of such communities can be overlooked: nor should it be forgotten that many things which, like honey or dogs, are nowadays luxuries, were once necessities, with a firm economic basis.

The negative aspect is as important as the positive. It is important to know the date of the introduction into a region of a plant or domesticated species, for we know then that in the preceding periods we do not have to reckon with it as an economic factor. Thus, it is important to know at what date the horse was introduced into these islands, and whether when introduced it was used for food, for riding, or for drawing carts or ploughs.[1] So far as I am acquainted with the evidence there is nothing to prove its presence here before the late Bronze Age.[2] Probably it was introduced

[1] The bones of the horse are of course the only direct proof of its presence during a given period. There are, however, many means of obtaining indirect evidence—the discovery of bits, bridle-pieces, and spurs and other adjuncts of horsemanship; of chariot wheels and their appurtenances; and of drawings or carved models of the horse. Other things are capable of being similarly tracked down by their characteristic implements—agriculture by the plough: hunting by the arrowhead, etc.

[2] Remains of the horse were not found in the neolithic portions of Wor Barrow.

by the leaf-shaped sword people who invaded Britain from the east towards the end of the Bronze Age.

All these, however, are points of detail. They do not often enter into archaeological work (except excavation), and they come more properly within the sphere of the naturalist who has been ' archaeologised ' on the lines suggested. But it is important that archaeologists should realise the value of restoring environmental factors (by whomever it may be done), not only for the completion of the picture or map they are reconstructing but also to impress their colleagues in other branches of science with the necessity of studying such matters. Whether they will succeed in doing so is another question. Archaeologists, for instance, have long been aware of the paramount need of expert geological assistance in the work of disentangling the subdivisions of the palaeolithic period. But, so far, that assistance has not been forthcoming in this country in anything like sufficient quantities. They can but go on trying to secure co-operation in this and in other matters. It should be clearly stated, for instance, that in any general treatment of the Bronze Age a vegetation map of the country at that time is urgently required, and that even an admittedly imperfect attempt would be better than none at all.

So far as the individual archaeologist is concerned, the importance of environment is, rather, an indirect one. For the greater part of his time he is engaged upon work of a detailed and technical character. It is only occasionally that he pauses to review in print a period as a whole from every point of view. But this general treatment should be present at the back of his mind throughout, as the ultimate aim of all research; and it would be summed up by a map which showed the physical environment of the time underlying and influencing the human distributions superimposed. His work will gain enormously in clarity, freshness and interest if he views it, down to the minutest detail of specialist research, against the background of human history as a whole, geographically portrayed.

CHAPTER XII

'VALUE' IN ARCHAEOLOGY

THE foregoing chapter suggests certain questions —Wherein lies the real value of archaeological specimens, and how can it be assessed? Are some of more value than others, and, if so, why?

Value, of course, depends entirely upon the use which will be made of the object concerned. What is of value to a man at one time may be of no value, and even an encumbrance, to him at another, and to others may never be of any value. A pith-helmet is useless to the member of an arctic expedition; but it is essential to the tropical explorer. A bronze axe casually found is useless to the finder who (as happens in nine cases out of ten) is ignorant of its very nature; but it is an important item in the armoury of the archaeologist. Now it should be observed that its value to him individually is a function, so to speak, of the use which he himself, as an archaeologist, can make of it; and that use will be greater or smaller in proportion to the width or narrowness of his outlook.[1] It is precisely here that the importance of thinking in terms of a map comes in. Isolated finds of single bronze implements can, if each is to be separately considered, add but little to knowledge; but when all are taken together and studied as a whole, and the distribution of every variety mapped, they can tell us an interesting story. And so with all other common archaeological objects, especially pottery. True, the exceptional find very often points the way; but generalisation from a single instance is to be eschewed.

I feel bound to emphasise this point very strongly, for I have come across so many instances where the value of isolated discoveries of common and familiar objects is regarded as unimportant even by archaeologists—who should know better; and I have often been put to considerable trouble in obtaining information which might easily have been recorded by them, but which they did not consider of sufficient importance. That was particularly true of the older school of archaeologists who flourished during the first half of the nineteenth

[1] But even if, on the other hand, he is not capable of extracting any use at all from it himself, he must not forget that others, perhaps as yet unborn, may be able to do so. Herein lies his obligation to leave as full a record of it as possible; for the body of knowledge is one, and unaffected by accidents of time or space. Accurately recorded first-hand evidence written down a hundred years ago is often as valuable as if it had been written yesterday, sometimes more so. Without a realisation of this continuity, knowledge would cease to advance.

century; they were often content to record the finding of a 'celt' (without further specification), and sometimes even failed to mention the site of its discovery. The site, of course, is, to the geographically minded archaeologist, of the very first importance; without it the object is valueless even to him, except in its time-aspect, as a link in the development of a type. Even so, it cannot be used unless at least the district in which it was found is known.

The moral is that every find of an archaeological nature should be fully recorded and illustrated as soon as possible after it is found. That was the principle upon which General Pitt-Rivers worked; and I cannot refrain from quoting some pertinent remarks of his.

'Common things', he says,[1] 'are of more importance than particular things, because they are more prevalent. I have always remembered a remark of Professor Huxley's in one of his addresses. "The word *importance*", he says, "ought to be struck out of scientific dictionaries; that which is important is that which is persistent." Common things vary in form, as the idea of them passes from place to place, and the date of them and of the places in which they are found may sometimes be determined by gradual variations of form. *There is no knowing what may hereafter be found to be most interesting* [italics mine]. Things apt to be overlooked may afterwards turn out to be of the greatest value in tracing the distribution of forms. This will be admitted when it is recognised that distribution is a necessary prelude to generalisation.'

[1] *Excavations in Cranborne Chase*, vol. iv., 1898, p. 27.

'VALUE' IN ARCHAEOLOGY

Distribution implies a map, and a map is the best of all generalisations, for it is at the same time a visible incarnation of all the particulars.

Let us then proceed to consider distribution more fully.

CHAPTER XIII

DISTRIBUTIONS

THE study of distributions is one which is likely to attract a good deal of attention in the immediate future; it is probable that most of the advances in archaeological knowledge will be made by means of geographical studies. It is therefore necessary to inquire somewhat at length into the scope and limitations of the distributional method.

For this purpose we must revert for a moment to the question of culture. Culture was defined as the sum total of all the activities of a community. Now, just as the archaeologist in his purely archaeological work of excavation and in his study of the evolution and classification of types is aiming at the discovery of homogeneous cultures, so in his geographical work he tries to discover the extent in space of each culture, its frontiers and its points of contact with other cultures. Further, he wishes to discover the original home of each culture, to trace its gradual expansion and the routes followed.

He is thus concerned with cultures immobile,

DISTRIBUTIONS

mobile and impinging. When considering the immobile aspects of a culture, he is concerned with the area occupied, the geographical influences of environment which determined the selection and frontiers of that area, the density or sparseness of the population, and the shifting 'centres of gravity' during the different epochs. To discover the area occupied by the culture he must select something which would not as a rule wander far from the home, such as earthen pots, or some quite immobile object, like a particular type of dolmen or chambered barrow. He will also learn a good deal by studying the distribution of types of homesteads or villages, where it is obvious that before the type can be determined a series of plans must be made.[1] (Anything which has an intimate connection with the social life of the community, such as burial customs, for instance, is of value in support of more material evidence, and is quite as capable of geographical treatment.) In all this kind of work the main difficulty lies in selecting the types beforehand: there are always so many examples which lie on the border-line and represent a transitional stage from one type to another. Type, moreover, is a complex of shape, texture and ornament, and it is difficult in classifying objects to estimate errors due to the personal equation. On the other hand, there is a danger in applying rigid mathematical tests,

[1] It is essential for purposes of comparison that these should all be reproduced on a uniform scale.

for they may fail to include obvious examples, and may include others which do not belong.

It is necessary to examine this question of the selection of types rather closely, for it lies at the root of all problems of distribution. If your types are open to criticism your whole work may be invalidated. Remember that for the moment we are dealing with the *immobile* aspect of culture; we are trying to determine the areas where the people of whom it was characteristic lived and moved and had their being. We are not for the present concerned with their trade or with their ultimate origins. What probably happens now, in default of any existing ' corpus ', is something like this. In visiting a number of provincial museums or private collections, one's eye is caught by some marked peculiarity in the prehistoric pottery or implements of a certain period — a peculiarity which appears to be a local (or rather a regional) development. As an instance may be given the straight-necked, round-bodied cinerary urns of the Late Bronze Age in Dorset with their characteristic decoration, and the straight-sided or barrel-shaped urns, with raised rib and sham handles, of South Central England. As examples of local types of bronze implements may be mentioned some types characteristic of South Dorset, the Hampshire Basin and Sussex. Having, probably in the way described, discovered the existence of a type, the next thing is to determine its age. This can only be done, to begin with, by hunting up in the Pro-

DISTRIBUTIONS

ceedings of the local scientific society (or elsewhere) the account of the discovery of at least one of the objects of the type in question and its associations. In the case of bronze implements, at least, the labels in the museum *should* tell one whether the discovery was an isolated one or whether it formed part of a hoard. If the latter, the other objects found in the hoard should help to fix its date. In any case, out of the total number of instances, enough evidence will probably be found to provide some clue to the authenticity of the type and to its regional or other development. The next step will be to study its evolution and distribution in the usual manner.

It will be noted that I have assumed that the types in question are provincial. Perhaps it would be more correct to call them 'sub-types' and to reserve the term 'types' for objects which are characteristic of larger areas. For certain objects are found distributed over the whole of the British Isles and along the opposite coasts of the Continent, all of them resembling each other so closely as to belong to the same type. Such, for instance, are gold lunulae, torques, bracelets and bronze leaf-shaped swords. It is obvious that the distribution of objects of this type must be studied on a different scale, so to speak, from those whose type varies from region to region. What is the fundamental distinction between these two classes of objects? Why is it that in the one case we may find a sword from the Thames almost identical in type with one

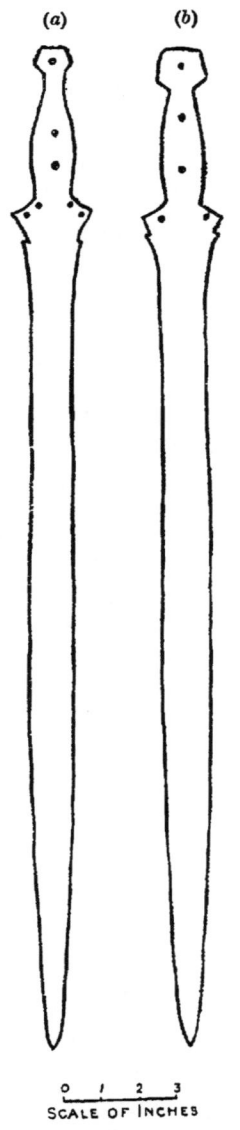

(a) Bronze sword found in the Thames, near Battersea; now in the British Museum.

(b) Bronze sword found on Haapa Kylä Heath, Nyland, Finland; now in the Helsingfors Museum.[1]

[1] See *Vorgeschichtliche Altertümer aus Finland* (Helsingfors, 1900), Plate XXXII., Fig. 4.

DISTRIBUTIONS

from Central Europe or Finland, whereas the axes used by the people of the Hampshire Basin were totally different from those used by their neighbours in Dorset and Sussex? The answer is quite clear. The sword type did not develop locally, whereas the axe and cinerary urn did. In the latter case there were opportunities for the development of regional characteristics which were absent in the former. It is thus possible to introduce a system of classification of objects according to their value as evidence of settlement areas, trade, migration and influence.

Beakers are a good example of that class of object whose distribution when mapped indicates the settlement areas of the people who made them. Here we have an article of everyday use, introduced fully developed by an invading people. As a rule it is very easy to recognise a beaker immediately at sight; it is only the later and degenerate forms that present any difficulties. Beakers are therefore of very great value in determining the great primary settlement areas of the people responsible for them. For in selecting and classifying types, one of the most difficult tasks is to decide where to draw the line between the early and middle forms and between the middle and late forms; and to distinguish between the crudeness of youth and the degeneracy of age. In the case of beakers there is no such difficulty, for the early forms are all absent. The development of the beaker took place on the

Continent, where, doubtless, the evolution of both shape and ornament may be traced from their earliest beginnings.

Flat copper and bronze axes are also useful in the same way as beakers; they have no earlier history, being the first metal axes ever made in this country; but there is considerable difficulty in drawing the line between the flat axe and that which has an incipient stop-ridge and side-flanges. Moreover it is by no means evident that the distinction, though important typologically, has any special significance for us when we are dealing with distributions; what we want is to discover settlement areas, and if, as is likely, both flat and flanged axes were in use at the same time or nearly so, there is not much sense in emphasising the distinction. It is not likely that the settlement areas would have been appreciably altered during the short period necessary for the development of flange or stop-ridge. This, however, remains to be proved. The dividing line has got to be drawn somewhere, and the principle of keeping one map for one type should be adhered to. Later on, some combined maps can easily be compiled to bring out certain features of distribution.

I mention these minor points which arise to show the difficulties which beset the path of the archaeologist when he is dealing with even so simple an object as a flat bronze axe. When he comes to deal with later and more complex types the difficulties increase a hundredfold. Take palstaves,

DISTRIBUTIONS

for example. It would of course be possible to map the distribution of all those which have been found in the British Isles. But it is certain that palstaves were in use over a long period of time, during which many changes may have taken place in the settlement areas of their users. Further, it is impossible without a good deal of preliminary study to classify the earlier types of palstave and to differentiate between them and the later types of flanged stop-ridge celts. A good deal of typological work is necessary before we can begin to study their distribution. It was because the need of a *corpus* was realised that a committee of the British Association (Section H) was formed in 1913 to study the distribution of metal objects of the Bronze Age. It was felt that the problem of the distribution of all the different types of gold and bronze objects over even so relatively small an area as the British Isles was incapable of solution by one or two isolated individuals. Co-operation was necessary to obtain in each single instance the drawings and other details by means of which alone comparisons can be made and types determined. Moreover it is essential to such an undertaking that the drawings shall be made on a uniform system and scale, for in assigning an object to its proper type, the brain works through the eye, and a mixture of scales inevitably leads to confusion, especially where one is dealing, as here, with a large mass of evidence. A standardised form of record and drawing was therefore agreed upon, and the whole results are being filed on the card-index system.

I believe this to be the ideal method of dealing with problems of distribution. It is applicable to every kind of object, and not merely to metal implements. I should like to see similar drawings (with photographs) of all the ancient skulls which have been found in barrows and cemeteries, with measurements of the femur and notes as to the type of tomb and burial and associated objects. A beginning might be made with skulls found in Long Barrows, and with the river-bed type; there are quite a number of the former scattered over the country (in local museums) which have never been properly described or illustrated. More would be bound to turn up in the course of the inquiry. I should also like to see started a card index of the megalithic monuments of Europe and North Africa and the adjacent regions;[1] it should be undertaken by national and provincial committees. On each card would be a plan, elevation and photograph of the dolmen or other structure, with details about any excavations, methodical or haphazard, which have been made in or around it. Cross references would be made to other card-index catalogues when necessary; for instance, it would be often necessary to give such references in the megalithic catalogue to the skulls found in Long Barrows. Pottery vessels should also be card-

[1] A Committee of the Royal Anthropological Institute has been formed for this purpose since I wrote this chapter.

DISTRIBUTIONS

indexed with a view to determining the origin of the people who made them and the regions where the types were evolved. In the absence of any such *corpus* of exact information the archaeologist is thrown back upon scattered scraps of evidence for the solution of the all-important problems of the wanderings of peoples, the spread of culture and ' influences ' and the routes followed by trade.

Some sort of system is essential in the working out of problems of distribution : for it must not be forgotten that we are primarily concerned, not with the objects themselves and their different types, but with the people who made them. They are only a means to an end, and the end is man : we approach him through his works. Now, culture being the sum total of all the activities of a community or group of communities, it is clear that we shall get only a partial glimpse of that culture by studying the distribution of a single one of its component elements. We must not, for instance, study the distribution of pottery without some time or another studying also the distribution of the implements (of stone or metal) used by the same people.[1] To know a culture thoroughly we should study the distribution of as many of its component parts as possible, such as pottery, implements and ornaments, weapons, burials and habitations. It is of the utmost importance that all who are

[1] For their pots will reveal to us the region where they lived, and their implements and ornaments will confirm this, and throw light on their commercial relations with other communities.

working, or who intend to start working, on the problems of distribution should realise this fact before they begin to draw conclusions from their work; otherwise these conclusions, being based on a *single* class of evidence, may be vitiated. We hope great things of our bronze implement survey when it is completed, but we must beware of expecting from it more than it can fairly yield.

It will be a good thing to consider in a general way what kind of conclusions may safely be drawn from different kinds of evidence. First, as regards gold and bronze implements. The vast majority of these consist of chance finds. This is especially true of axes, which have only in a few cases been found by archaeological excavation in barrows and other earthworks. The implements, whether isolated specimens or hoards, have usually been discovered by labourers—digging in the ground to make a hole for a gate-post, making a trench for a sewer, making a field drain, laying the foundations of a house, digging out a fox or badger, grubbing a tree, removing a boulder, draining a marsh, making a pond, laying out a garden, digging for peat, quarrying and so on. Dredging in river-beds has also been responsible for a large number of finds, particularly near London. Now, looking at it from the point of view of the student who is going to draw conclusions from the evidence of these finds taken as a whole and regarded geographically, we have to consider two things—the manner in which these objects were originally lost, and the causes which have operated to bring them to light again. In the case of single specimens it is probable that accident was always responsible for their loss. That being so, we should expect to find a fair sprinkling of implements on our map over areas which were inhabited contemporaneously and also along the lines of trade-routes. The law of probabilities determines that the greatest number of implements will have been lost within the inhabited area, and that outside the area the percentage of losses will be highest along the routes followed by trade. Where trade-routes traverse settlement areas the proportion of finds will probably be greater in the vicinity of the trade-route than elsewhere in the region. That is because the bronze implements were probably procured from traders using those very routes; the people who lived alongside them would be more likely to be well supplied with their goods than those who lived some distance away. Further, a trade-route or highway always increases the prosperity of the communities through whose territory it passes, and creates a belt of slightly denser population along its course; and the denser the population the more numerous will be their losses—and our discoveries.

In the early days, when we were just beginning to discover the fascination of these problems, we used to spend much time in constructing imaginary trade-routes across the map by joining up a line of finds. Such a trade-route was that from Christchurch *via* Salisbury Plain and the Upper Severn

Valley to North Wales and Ireland. Now I would not wish it to be understood that I disbelieve in the existence of a trade-route along some such course as that described. But I wish to point out certain crudities in our methods. We were a little too prone to confuse two distinct processes — the tracking of an old road on foot across country, and the theoretical reconstruction of a line of communication upon the map, from many kinds of data. We assumed that it was possible to restore the exact course of the road by plotting on a map the sites of chance finds of bronze implements. This is rather too rash an assumption. It suggests the picture of a kind of prehistoric paper-chase, where the trail was laid by a pedlar scattering his goods. One imagines him shouldering his pack at Christchurch or Holyhead, and dropping the contents at fords and cross-roads for the benefit of his archaeological pursuer. The evidence was forced to tell more than it contained.

Of course, there is this much to be said on the other side, that if a trade-route did exist and was used by travelling pedlars, objects would certainly be lost from time to time — the pedlar himself would be drowned, or bogged, or killed by a fall of timber or a wild beast, and his goods would perish with him. Moreover such catastrophes would happen more often at crucial and convergent points, in crossing a river or marsh or in penetrating a thick forest. Fortunately a discovery has recently been made which illustrates this very well. A hoard consisting of broken fragments of swords and spearheads was found in the marshes of the so-called ' Anton ' stream just above Andover, at exactly the point where it is crossed by an undoubted ancient trade-route called the Harroway. Here is an almost certain case of a pedlar losing his goods through the difficulty of crossing alluvial ground. There is no suspicion here of question-begging, since the exact course of the Harroway is known here to a yard, and was known long before the hoard was discovered.

The reason why I am a little suspicious of the 'line of finds', and of the direct inferences drawn from it, is that I expect these single isolated finds will prove eventually to be the nuclei of small groups of similar or contemporary objects, which will then indicate the existence of settlements, or small settlement areas at these places. In the case of finds in or near a large river we must also bear in mind that there are two possible explanations of their presence there. They may be due either to the passage of a trade-route *across* the river, or to the penetration of traders and settlers *up* it. Rivers whose course is not enveloped by marsh for any considerable length on both sides —whose banks, therefore, are occasionally formed of firm gravel suitable for landing on—must always have attracted settlers. Subsequent communication between different riverine communities would be mostly by boat, and objects would thus be bartered from village to village. These conditions would obtain where a large river flows through forest country. Villages would cluster along its banks and along those of its tributaries, and would be situated at favourable landing-places. They would be often cut off from each other by land, but intercourse would be maintained by water in boats or canoes. Goods would be obtained from a seaport near the mouth of the river, and would pass up-stream from one village to another.[1] Such is my impression of the conditions which obtained, at any rate at the beginning of the Bronze Age, in the lower reaches of the Severn, and possibly to some extent in the lower Thames Basin and round the mouth of the Medway. The same may also have been true of the estuaries of Devon and Cornwall, such as those of the Tamar and the Fal.

We shall derive much help in studying the course of trade-routes if we bear in mind the risk of relying too much upon a single class of evidence. It has been said that pottery is the best evidence for determining settlement areas. These need not be of great extent; they may not be much bigger than a large parish. Let us imagine for a moment that all our card-index catalogues are complete. We find that a number of small settlement areas emerge, isolated from each other, and situated at favourable spots in regions which consist for the most part of marsh, forest, or barren scrub

[1] In the south of England *land*-communication may often have been possible and sometimes even preferable: the lower Avon valley is a case in point, for special reasons to be described later.

and heath. We are able further to differentiate between these small settlement areas, and to distinguish those which were prosperous from those which were not—to select, in fact, those which could purchase gold and bronze objects and finely worked flint implements. In other words, we can distinguish between the centres and backwaters of primitive culture. We must also bear in mind, all the time, that in such regions the discovery of, say, a single gold object is *representative*, standing for a number which were lost, and either never found again or found and melted down. We shall be safe in concluding that those areas, both large and small, where large numbers of finds have been made of imported objects or objects made of imported material, were situated on the route of trade between two distinct regions—if, of course, they were not themselves the goal of trade. This conclusion will be safe if there is no possibility of the objects or their raw material being obtained locally.

Having resolved our rather too precisely defined trade-route into a vaguer but more reliable ' line of trade ', we are at liberty to speculate upon the exact course followed. Such speculations are most fascinating and are quite legitimate, provided we realise the uncertainties and pitfalls with which they are beset. There are quite a number of sign-posts to keep the constructive imagination of archaeologists upon the right track. They are mainly topographical, and will be dealt with in the chapter on Old Roads. Direct archaeological evidence is provided by the existence of ancient tracks and by well-authenticated and located finds like that near Andover just described.

A great deal of prehistoric trade was probably sea-borne; of that which went overland some probably consisted of bartering from one settlement to another; however, where settlements were widely scattered, or separated by large tracts of uninhabited country, a regular trade may have been carried on by pedlars who hawked their goods from place to place, and who may have thus covered quite long distances. The routes they followed would at first be the tracks connecting one settlement with the next; but if the trade continued for any length of time the tracks so used would tend to acquire an importance over the rest, and in due course a kind of trunk road would grow up. Most of our main roads have come into existence by the connecting up of lesser roads leading from one village or market-town to another. The question of the exact means by which goods were conveyed from one place to another is beyond the scope of the present chapter and is immaterial to it. For the moment we are concerned only with the existence of certain lines of trade which can be traced by the distribution of objects along its course. So far I have dealt only in generalities. I have, however, had in mind certain parts of England where illustrative instances occur.

One such trade-route which suggested itself

DISTRIBUTIONS 149

from the distributions mapped in my Bronze Age paper[1] was that going from Warrington near the mouth of the Mersey to Peterborough. The evidence for a small group of settlements at both these places was very good, and at Peterborough the actual remains of a settlement were found. Both these places were favourably situated for use as ports by prehistoric navigators. I do not know enough about the regional archaeology of the districts in question to say whether any other inhabited site existed in the neighbourhood during the Early Bronze Age, but there can be no doubt of the existence and prosperity of these two ports. They lie at the two terminal points of a route which crosses England at one of its narrowest places, so that any trade between Ireland on the west and Scandinavia, Germany or the Netherlands on the east would have been quite likely to follow it. My reason, however, for quoting this instance is concerned not with the ports, but with a large settlement area crossed by this trade-route, namely, the Peak District. It will be seen from both the maps illustrating my paper referred to above, that the Peak District was one of the most clearly defined settlement areas in Britain. Its exact limits are the same as those of the carboniferous limestone. Considered as a beaker-making area, it compares well with Salisbury Plain, though the latter is rather richer. But when we compare the number of flat bronze axes found in the two

[1] See p. 80.

regions we find that a far greater number have been found in the northern area than in the southern. That this is not due to the disturbing influence of any accidental factor is certain, for I have tested the circumstances of their discovery and preservation. It is therefore probably due to the position of this region athwart the course of a trade-route between Ireland, the home of the flat axe, and the Continent. The discovery of only a few gold objects within the area confirms this explanation; it is not likely that the inhabitants of a barren limestone region would be as well able to purchase expensive ornaments as would the rich agricultural inhabitants of Salisbury Plain: and the humbler axe would be of far more value to them as a means of defence against wolves and other wild beasts.

We conclude, therefore, that pottery is to be the chief guide in determining the settlement areas during any period, while metal objects are the best clues for trade. Of course the distribution of megalithic monuments and burial-places is an even better guide to settlement areas than pottery, but in many cases it is only from the pottery associated with them that we can assign a date to them. This is true of barrows, with the exception of Long Barrows, which belong exclusively to the neolithic period. We do not yet know enough to say precisely to what age belong the various megalithic monuments, such as dolmens, stone-circles and monoliths. When the megalithic card index is complete we shall have a mass of evidence, sufficient probably to determine their age in the various regions where they occur; for it is not certain that they are contemporary even over the small area of the British Isles. In inferring trade from the presence of the bronze implements we are on sure ground, for we know that the actual objects which are found in the region devoid of all natural ores *must* have been introduced from outside.

So far I have dealt only with the land aspects of trade, but it is probable that a great proportion of the trade was sea-borne. My reason for so thinking is the abundance of hoards of bronze implements upon the sea-coast and round the estuaries of navigable rivers. I have not got the exact figures, but it will be sufficient to point out that, while in the two counties of Berks and Wilts (the latter very thickly inhabited in prehistoric times) only two hoards have ever been found, in Hampshire and the Isle of Wight their number is nearly twenty, of which only four were found inland. The same is true of the Dorset coast, the Sussex coast, and the estuaries of the Thames and Medway, where an enormous number of hoards have been found. A glance at Déchelette's map of hoards found in France shows that they occur far more thickly round the mouths of rivers like the Garonne and the Loire and in the Cotentin peninsula than elsewhere. This points to the conclusion that the raw copper and tin, having been brought by sea from Cornwall and Ireland, was made into axes and other implements by the people on the coast. They in turn would pass on their finished goods to the inhabitants of the hinterland. We may thus expect to find a number of trade-routes leading from ports to settlement areas inland. We may also speculate upon the sea-routes followed by traders.

In addition to commerce there is another process at work which affects the form and style of objects characterising a given culture. It is the *influence* exercised upon it by adjacent cultures with which intercourse is or has been maintained. The detecting of this influence is one of the most delicate tasks of the archaeologist. All the more important, therefore, it is to know exactly what we mean when we are dealing with this elusive wanderer. Let me take an instance. The existence of cinerary urns with broad handles in Cornwall has been cited as a case of 'Breton influence'. Now, what exactly does this mean? It is clearly not intended to mean that any single urn was made in Brittany and exported to Cornwall. It may mean that the people who made these urns had at one time or other learnt their trade from the people of Brittany who habitually made urns with broad handles; or, more probably, that the ancestors of these people acquired the habit (whether in Brittany or Cornwall) and transmitted it to their descendants. Thus the Cornish people of that period would be cousins of the Bretons, both being descended from a common broad-handled-urn-making ancestor.

This ancestral stock would thus have migrated and by degrees populated Cornwall and Brittany; there they would carry on their custom of making urns with broad handles. After a time the urns, too, would differentiate from the parent stock and form new regional varieties, but the broad handle would remain, like a rudimentary organ, to provide us with a clue to the pedigree of the type.

CHAPTER XIV

OLD ROADS AND LINES OF COMMUNICATION

IT is not within the scope of this book to deal with any region or period except in illustration of some principle or method of archaeological research. In this chapter the dominant factor is *position*, which may be considered both statically and dynamically. Statically, position is concerned only with the location of a community or a group of communities on the earth's surface. Dynamically, it is concerned with the relation of a community to its natural environment in so far as that environment affects its intercourse with other communities. We shall therefore be concerned with the latter aspect—with 'people in motion'. Illustrations, as usual, will mainly be taken from Wessex.

Wessex as a province of England consists of the chalk district of south central England and the tertiary area of the Hampshire basin and part of the London basin—roughly, the counties of Hants, Berks, Wilts and Dorset. Starting from the Goring Gap, it is bounded on the north and west by the chalk escarpments of the Berkshire

Downs, the Marlborough Downs and Salisbury Plain, and the Dorset escarpments overlooking the Vale of Blackmore. On the east it is bounded by the Thames from Goring to Reading and then by the line of the railway from Reading to Farnham; then by a line drawn southwards from Farnham to Chichester. Between Reading and Farnham the frontier is indeterminate; farther south it is formed by the chalk scarp which forms the western limit of the Weald. On the south it is bounded by the sea. The Isle of Wight is of course included. In prehistoric times this area comprised an open undulating down-land of which Salisbury Plain is typical. Where the chalk was covered with clay the close turf of the downs gave place to a ranker growth interspersed with heather, bracken, gorse, and even thorns and stunted oaks. The tertiary districts were mostly barren heathland, with dense forests covering the lower clay-lands. In the main, however, Wessex was open grass-land, and the chalk districts were well adapted for agriculture.

This open region was hemmed in by an almost continuous belt of forest and waste land encircling it on every side. On the north was the sodden plain of the Vale of the White Horse. On the west were the clay forests of Selwood and Gillingham, joining on the south to the Vale of Blackmore, a region very like the Vale of the White Horse. On the north-east were the wooded slopes of the Chilterns and the eastern parts of Berkshire round Bradfield; then came the London clay forests south of Reading. On the eastern margin of Hampshire were the Wealden clay forests. In Hampshire itself the eastern chalk uplands formed a difficult country of clay-topped hills covered with dense scrub and intersected by innumerable steep-sided valleys. This double barrier extended almost to the sea. The scrub lands of both eastern Berks and Hants gradually thinned out westwards into open grass down-land.

This forest belt encircled Wessex like the thorny hedge which guarded the castle of the Sleeping Beauty. It was breached in four places by natural land-bridges connecting Wessex with the outer world. To them were added two others where man has completed the breach begun by nature. On the southern side the sea-wall was, so to speak, breached by a number of excellent harbours, admirably suited to the needs of prehistoric navigators, so far as one can guess at what their requirements were.

I have called these breaches 'land-bridges'; but the term is more applicable to a natural causeway across a flat marshy region, and the obstacle in question is not marsh but impenetrable forest. The breaches in this forest are like passes in a mountain-range, and I shall therefore call them 'forest-passes'. The principal is that which leads across the Test-Blackwater divide at Basingstoke to the Hog's Back. Then comes that which connects the Berkshire Downs with the Chilterns, by the Thames crossing at Goring. Then there is the

OLD ROADS

northern entrance across the Thames-Avon divide at Wootton Bassett. A fourth but less important (for reasons which will appear) is that which leads along the South Downs from Winchester through Droxford and across Butser into Sussex. In addition to these natural passes, man has broken through the forest in two other places, through Selwood Forest, over the watershed at Witham, and across Blackmore Vale at Yeovil.

In estimating the influence of natural position upon the cultural development of a people we must keep two facts clear. When we are dealing with a large area like Wessex, it is clear that the primary factor is the absence of forests and marsh—the existence of a large open area where a pastoral or agricultural community could settle without impediment. In due course, as culture advanced and social life and intercourse began to develop, the subsidiary factors of position (such as forest-passes to other regions) would make themselves felt. We must, however, beware of the conception of the Early Bronze Age chieftain starting out for these shores, map in hand, and pondering over the relative advantages of Wessex and East Anglia, and finally deciding on Wessex because of the advantages provided by its geographical position for trade and intercourse with distant lands. Of course, nothing of the kind occurred. Nevertheless, the open areas would certainly be filled up and populated first, and those of them which possessed more geographical advantages than others would in due course benefit by them, but not until the inhabitants had reached the pitch of culture necessary to appreciate and make use of those natural endowments.

The process is well illustrated by the case of Wessex. Here we have a large open area which in prehistoric times was thickly populated, and reached a fairly high level of culture as early as the beginning of the Bronze Age, when Stonehenge was probably built. Nowhere else probably in England did there exist so large an area with a uniformly dense population. As the process of clearing the forests advanced, Wessex lost its former compactness, while it still retained its supremacy. Gradually, however, the tide of agriculture has swept away the old provincial frontiers, and Wessex no longer exists as a corporate organism in the social scheme. The invention of the steam-engine and the discovery of the use of coal for fuel have shifted the centre of gravity from south to north. Coal was there all the time, but it did not begin to exercise anthropogeographical influence until man on his side acquired the skill necessary for exploiting it. Thus has ' civilisation ' from time immemorial been made up of two elements — man and his environment.

Wessex in the Early Bronze Age must have been the centre of gravity of England, to which all roads led. From the north-east along the Ridgeway came traders bringing amber from the Baltic or east coast, and perhaps, also, some of the finer products of the Fenland flint industry. From the south and west came Cornish tin and copper and the products of maritime trade. Through the forest-pass of Witham there came, in later times, the Mendip lead, along the route followed by the Roman road. Eastwards along the Harroway intercourse was kept up, at any rate during the Late Bronze Age, with the people living on the southern shores of the Thames estuary: south-eastwards, with the miners of Cissbury and the people of the

Bronze dagger, 7⅛ in. long, found on Winterbourne Bassett Down, Wilts; now in the Museum of the Wiltshire Archaeological Society at Devizes.[1]

Sussex coast-lands. The existence of trade-relations [2] with so many distant regions points to a fairly high state of culture at the central mart, such as we actually find in the Early Bronze Age barrows round Stonehenge. It also throws an interesting sidelight on the origin of both Stonehenge itself and its prototype Avebury. For Avebury is situated close to the junction of the Ridgeway (coming from Fenland along the crest of the

[1] See *Catalogue of the Museum*, Part II., 1911, p. 26; Plate XIII., Fig. 5.
[2] All of these have not yet been established, and any remarks here are intended to be taken rather as suggestions than as statements of fact. The existence of the trade-routes in question is however rendered highly probable by evidence which cannot be detailed here. For the gold trade see my article on the Early Bronze Age, *Geographical Journal*, 1912.

Berkshire and Marlborough Downs) with the gold route, coming across the Wootton Bassett divide. Similarly Stonehenge lies at the exact point where the Harroway (coming from Cornwall and making for the Thames estuary) is crossed by the gold route on its way to Christchurch *via* the lower Avon valley. Stonehenge is also the point to which the other trade-routes described all converge. It is not, of course, suggested that either of these monuments was built to commemorate this convergence, but rather that a definite but indirect connection exists between them and the geographic and economic factors involved. In matters of religion, cause and effect are often inextricably confused. It is to the interests of an established church [1] to encourage trade and thereby ally itself with temporal authority, and the promotion of pilgrimages is one of the surest means to this end. The building of the Mahdi's tomb by the wily Khalifa Abdullah at Omdurman, the great mart of the Sudan, is a case in point.

The extraordinary abundance of barrows on Salisbury Plain, and especially in the immediate vicinity of Stonehenge, points also to the existence of a large population. We have seen that there are good geographical reasons for this in Wessex. Now when we get a large population with a thriving system of commerce and a seaboard provided with

---

[1] That is, a church whose religion has the united support of the people and their rulers, as have nearly all religious organisations amongst primitive peoples. It is only with the spread of education and its dissociation from a priestly caste that dissent begins.

suitable harbours, we shall be sure to find that maritime trade will develop. Ports will spring up round the harbours and land trade-routes will lead to them; for, after all, a port is only the meeting-place of many routes by land and sea, the coastal equivalent of the market-town. If we take the coast-line of Wessex as extending from Portland Bill on the west to Selsea Bill on the east, and including the Isle of Wight, we shall find that most of the important ports of prehistoric times are found within these limits. Actual figures are difficult in the present state of knowledge, but I have made a rough estimate of the number of prehistoric ports between Land's End and Romney Marsh, and it appears that the Wessex Coast embraces about half of them, though its coast-line is only about a quarter of the whole in length. Similarly, in Roman times the proportion is the same. Why is it that the countless creeks and harbours along the coasts of Devon and Cornwall were so little used? The reason is that they had no crowded hinterland of wealthy communities. Neither barren upland nor wooded valley was capable of supporting more than a scanty pastoral population. The natural endowments of stone and metals were not enough in themselves to give rise in early days to a dense population. For primitive man cannot increase and multiply without an abundant food-supply from close at hand. He must support himself and his family mainly from the region he inhabits. Nowadays we are less dependent upon an immediate source of food-supply, though the risks we thereby run will not need to be recounted to this generation. Yet the big ports still hover round the edges of areas of dense population. Setting aside naval dockyards, the largest amount of tonnage is registered at ports like Leith, Glasgow and Liverpool, Hull and London, all dominated by the influence of adjacent industrial areas. These, in their turn, derive from coalfields, and so we come back to this, that coal exercises to-day the same indirect control over maritime commerce as was exercised in the Bronze Age by agriculture—or, if this be considered unproven, we may equally well substitute for agriculture favourable conditions for pastoral life.

CHAPTER XV

ROMAN ROADS : GENERAL METHODS AND ARCHAEO-
LOGICAL EVIDENCE

IN all scientific work specialisation is necessary. That does not mean that the scientific worker must spend his whole time in a single narrow groove; far from it. But without a groove he will do no good either to himself or to the world at large. As an example of specialist research in archaeology I have chosen Roman roads, mainly because it is, for the time being, my own particular groove; partly also because of the popular interest which Roman roads excite; and partly because the subject-matter is a concrete, visible thing—a raised causeway, now more or less decayed. Further, the business of tracing these roads is simple, requiring no outfit beyond a sharp pair of eyes, a pencil and a six-inch map. Nor can the field archaeologist, however inexperienced, by any possibility do harm to the roads he is tracing. Field archaeology is thus very different from excavation, which should never be attempted by the novice without expert assistance; and it forms an admirable and indispensable preparation for spade-work. It trains the powers of observation and judgement; it strengthens the critical faculties; and it develops a precise habit of mind. For entries recorded upon a map at the moment of observation preclude all possibility of vagueness or hedging, and compel rapid and more or less irrevocable decisions. That is why map-work in archaeology is superior to mere description alone; for behind the subtleties of verbiage the author may conceal a culpable lack of discrimination and other shortcomings.

Of all branches of field archaeology the study of Roman roads is one of the most fascinating; nor is it true, as often assumed by those unfamiliar with the subject, that it is worked out. That will, I think, be clear from what follows.

In the south of England, and probably elsewhere, the Romans made their roads as far as possible of local material. They only paved them with flagstones where a supply was obtainable close at hand. The Roman roads of Wessex were never paved. In chalk country they made them of flints quarried direct from the chalk. In tertiary country they usually made them from plateau and valley gravel. In one instance, that of the New Forest road ending at Lepe on the Solent, Dr. Williams-Freeman and I found hollow pits on either side of the road which appeared to have been made by the constructors to obtain material. The road itself is exceptionally well preserved there, upon a gravelly common. It appears as a broad raised causeway,

SECTION ACROSS ROMAN ROAD AT LATCHMORE GREEN,
1½ MILES SOUTH OF SILCHESTER.

The prong is resting on the flint causeway.

overgrown, of course, by heather, but still most distinct. A similar line of pits exists along the Roman road from Marlborough to Bath over Calstone Down.

The Roman engineers usually laid out their roads from one hill-top to another. Probably they did this at night, by means of fires, or by day through their smoke. Remains of charcoal were found *under* a Roman road in Chute Park in the eighteenth century.[1] At this point the road runs on very high ground, from which it can be seen at the present day as far as Winchester, running straight as a die the whole way. But northwards it turns just beyond the point where the charcoal was found. It will generally be observed that the turning-points occur at hills, not necessarily very high, but with an unimpeded view in the required directions. The deviation from the straight is often very slight : as far as possible the roads were laid out in a straight line from one town to another. When this was not possible a number of mutually intervisible points were selected, and the road was laid out in straight sections between them.

Roman roads ignore physical features in the south of England, unless they absolutely refuse to be ignored. It was laid down apparently in the Roman ' K.R.' that a road must run as nearly as possible in a straight line between the two places it connected, and straight it went over hill and

[1] *Archaeologia*, viii., 1787, 'Mr. Willis on the Ikeneld Street', p. 90, note f.

dale. The Lepe road, above referred to, by the slightest deviation would have kept along the top of the plateau to its termination at Lepe, and so have avoided the necessity of crossing a succession of awkwardly steep-sided gullies. But it does not do so. Red tape seems to be no modern invention. There are places, however, where the valleys are very deep and the sides too steep even for a Roman road to negotiate. It was then necessary to make a detour and pick up the old line again farther on. This is what happens in the case of the road from Marlborough to Winchester at Chute. The Roman road makes a great curve which has been known from time immemorial as Chute Causeway. The road from Winchester to Porchester, as it climbs Deacon Hill, follows a curved course for the same reason. Such deviations are uncommon, but should be watched for.

It must never be forgotten that the one thing which distinguishes a Roman road from almost all others is the existence of an artificial raised causeway, formed by rough flints or gravel in regions where this material occurs.[1] Unless there are some remains of this causeway, or evidence of its former existence, *at some point in its course*, it is not possible to consider a road as being of

---

[1] Causeways of this nature were not again made in England until quite recent times. There is therefore no difficulty in distinguishing them from Roman roads, unless they coincide with the suspected course of the latter. In such a case the *existing* causeway is sometimes of modern date, and, being broader than that of the Roman road, has usually obliterated it.

undoubted Roman origin. But a single authentic well-preserved fragment is enough, even if it be only a few yards in length. It is for the want of this that many so-called Roman roads are not really Roman at all. They may be *ancient* roads, pre-Roman, Anglo-Saxon or Mediaeval in date; they may have been used in Roman times; but they are not Roman roads unless they can be proved to conform with Roman methods of construction. In other words, they must run in straight sections when this is not physically impossible, and they must provide the evidence of an artificial raised causeway at, at least, one point in each sector.

It is necessary to state this very clearly because of the tendency to confuse Roman roads with tracks of prehistoric origin which may have been in use in Roman times. In a sense, of course, such tracks are Roman, if they existed and were used during the Roman occupation of Britain. But they are distinct in origin and character from Roman roads in the sense in which the term is used in this book, and indeed universally amongst archaeologists—to denote roads of Roman construction. The so-called Icknield Way and Ridgeway have often been termed Roman, but there is not a trace of a causeway to be found anywhere on their course: neither do they anywhere run in a straight line. On the contrary, they move in sinuous curves across the country, obeying all the laws of ancient trackways which have grown under the feet of those who first formed them. Nowhere do either of these roads betray the smallest signs of Roman handiwork. The Harroway in Hampshire, and the better known Pilgrim's Way, are both ancient roads of non-Roman origin, and I do not remember ever to have seen them described as Roman; but no doubt they have often been so described.

By way of explaining the way to discover the course of a Roman road where it has been lost, I propose to describe how I actually picked up the trail myself on several occasions. I shall do so because a narration of the facts as they really occurred is more likely to be of help to future workers than general statements of a didactic nature.

One of the first Roman roads I ever attempted to trace was that running from the Roman station of Cunetio, at Folly Farm, near Marlborough, to Old Sarum. Its course is marked for a short distance on the O.S. six-inch map as it passes through the enclosure of Braydon Hook in Savernake Forest, and it was described by Colt Hoare and marked by him on his map for a longer distance than on the O.S. map. In this case the documentary evidence of the two maps, old and new, made it clear that both Colt Hoare and the government surveyor (prompted probably by him) had found some visible evidence of a Roman road. It seemed, therefore, worth while exploring the neighbourhood with the object of prolonging the small six-inch map fragment in either direction. Starting at each end in turn it was not difficult to do this. I lost it soon after it emerged from the forest on the south.

I was less successful with a small fragment of the Cunetio-Spinae road close by. The course of this road is wholly lost between Seven Barrows Hill, near East Kennet, on the west, and Leverton cross-roads, north of Hungerford, on the east. A small fragment is marked on the six-inch O.S. map between Folly Farm and Stitchcombe, as ' supposed Roman road '. It is only about a quarter of a mile in length, and runs diagonally down the southern side of the Kennet Valley. It does not appear to be known, and is seldom referred to in books and papers which deal with Roman roads. It is, however, quite authentic, and is of great value, for it is the only trace we have of this missing portion, and it lies about in the middle of it. I was able to follow the road for a short distance westwards towards the bottom of the valley, but eastwards it is lost in land which has long been under cultivation.[1]

In both these cases I was first put on the right track by the six-inch O.S. map. It is always advisable to consult this, for the older school of antiquaries neglected it and often cast suspicion on its identifications. My experience has been that anything which the Ordnance Surveyor calls a Roman road is worth examining. It often proves to be such; but even if it does not, it may very likely be some-

[1] During the winter of 1919 I recovered portions of it in Hen Wood.

thing else not without interest for the field archaeologist. The sapper is a practical fellow who uses his eyes, and he does not as a rule mark anything that he cannot see plainly. Where he goes wrong the error can usually be brought home to some perverse antiquary who has misled him. If, on the other hand, the sapper is correct, the field archaeologist will often be able to follow the course of the road farther on where the sapper could not, for the field archaeologist has a trained eye for such work, and he uses evidence of many kinds which the sapper cannot be expected to know of. What this evidence consists in will be seen later, when we come to describe the work of tracing Roman roads in the field.

In addition to the published sheets of the six-inch O.S. map, there are kept at Southampton the original manuscript sheets from which the first edition of the one-inch map of England was engraved. These sheets were drawn on a scale of two inches to the mile, and they show many things which the published engraved edition omits. Through the courtesy of the Director-General I was enabled to examine these sheets. I obtained several valuable clues from them. One of the most helpful was that which showed the course of the Bitterne-Chichester road from Bitterne itself to Netley Common. Up till then it had been assumed that the Roman road followed a more southerly course, crossing the Meon estuary at Bursledon and following roughly the line of the

Southampton-Fareham-Chichester main road. Now I had long regarded this identification with suspicion, principally because it had not a single fragment of reliable evidence to support it: also because it was not in many places even approximately straight, and everywhere its alignment was un-Roman and unconvincing in appearance; and, finally, because it made the Roman road cross the Hamble estuary well below high-water mark. I do not know a single case where a Roman road does this in the area I have explored. Such a crossing would necessitate the building of a bridge, or the use of a ferry; and the latter would be a hindrance to the rapid movement of large bodies of troops. The Romans seem always to have preferred to make their roads cross just at or above high-water mark, where the river could be forded, or where a very small bridge would be enough. Armed, then, with the evidence of the old one-inch sheets, I set out to see if I could find any traces of the road still surviving where it was marked on the map more than a hundred years ago. Sure enough I found a long stretch of it on Netley Common, where the causeway was quite unmistakable. A little hunting through strawberry-fields and cottage-gardens enabled me to verify the whole course and reinsert it on the six-inch map.

I was baffled, however, eastwards; and neither the accounts of Leman nor field work enabled me to find it. Further investigations in the field are required, and any one with the necessary leisure may have better luck. It was, however, plain that the old theory of its course was quite wrong, and it remained to evolve a new one for the easterly portion. Taking the modern one-inch map I examined the course of the road westwards from its Chichester terminus. It looked as if the old theory was correct in identifying it with the modern Fareham-Chichester road up to a point; but at a certain point, at Bedhampton, the modern highroad makes a sharp bend from W.N.W. to W.S.W. Now, as has been explained, Roman roads rarely do this, unless compelled to do so by some natural obstacle, and there is no such obstacle here. So far so good; let it be assumed then that (1) the modern Chichester-Fareham road coincides with the course of the ancient Roman road as far as Bedhampton, and (2) that the Roman road was continued in the same straight line west-north-westwards for an unknown distance. Acting on these assumptions, I took ruler and pencil and drew a straight line on the one-inch map, producing the line of the Chichester-Bedhampton road. I found that it connected up two straight pieces of modern road, one near Purbrook and the other between Wine Cross and Lodge Farm in Boarhunt parish; and the course as thus hypothetically mapped showed many minor signs of authenticity. The line coincided with the northern boundary of Southwick Park and that of a small copse to the north-west of it, as well as with fragments of the southern boundary of Southwick parish on the straight piece of road near Purbrook. I therefore prolonged my line to Wickham Common, marked where the line crossed it, and visited the spot. There, in the very place where my pencil line went, and seven miles from its starting-point at Bedhampton, I found unmistakable remains of a Roman causeway in the bracken! I was able to follow it up eastwards as far as Belmont, where it comes into the line of the Chichester road.[1] Westwards towards Bitterne I have not yet recovered its course.

It is not often that one's working hypotheses are so successful. But without them one would often be at a loss to know where to start. When one is left with no evidence at all, the only thing to do is to take a map and to construct the best hypothesis that stray indications suggest. Having done so, the places where the road is most likely to be preserved are tracts which have never been under plough, like Wickham Common, or which have not been under cultivation within recent years, like large woods. It is not often that the first theory is correct. More often it is the fifth, sixth or seventh! The alternative course to setting up a hypothesis and testing it is to examine laboriously every field, and this is bound to involve a lot of fruitless labour—fruitless, that is, as regards the immediate objective, for field work with a six-inch map and pencil is never wholly barren of results. The hypothesis method is quite a legitimate one, and is fully justified by its results. It is only

[1] See folding map at end, "A Typical Roman Road."

dangerous when used by persons who are more anxious to prove their theories correct than to arrive at the truth. Theories are like nine-pins, set up to be tested by the ball of fact. The unstable ones will fall and the rest remain.

The course of the Roman road which ran southwards out of Winchester through St. Cross, along the western side of the Itchen Valley, was not known beyond Otterbourne Hill. It was generally assumed that it led to Bitterne, but no certain traces of it had been discovered south of Otterbourne Park Wood. I was anxious to investigate the Roman roads in this region, and, accordingly, I set about examining all the old maps of the district in my possession. On an old map of the country round Southampton, published in *Paterson's Roads* (16th edition, by Edward Mogg; London, 1822), the contemporary Bradshaw and Baedeker combined, I saw a hatched causeway marked on Chilworth Common. On referring to the old published edition of the one-inch Ordnance Map I saw that this causeway was there faintly indicated. I visited the spot and was able to verify the existence of a Roman road there by unmistakable evidence, and subsequently to trace its course as far as Nursling. It was then quite clear that this road was not making for Bitterne, but for the New Forest, and probably ultimately for Poole.[1] In

[1] It is not, however, clear yet whether a branch road may have gone on to Bitterne. I have failed to find any certain traces of such a road, but the accounts of earlier investigators seem to point

ROMAN ROADS

the neighbourhood of Nursling it is difficult to trace, and I have not so far been able to discover with certainty the exact point where it crosses the Test. It probably does so near the high-water mark of ordinary tides at Nursling Mill, where a Roman settlement existed, in a field called Armsea.

West of the Test Valley a Roman road had been described by Hatcher,[1] and I found many valuable hints in Leman's manuscript. Later writers had vaguely grasped the fact that some remains of a road had been found near Copythorne in the New Forest, and had attempted to connect it with an imaginary road to Bitterne along the northern boundary of Southampton Common and elsewhere. But none of these writers took the trouble to test their theories in the field, and the whole question of these roads between the Itchen and the Test had got into a state of hopeless confusion. The discovery of a road from Winchester to Nursling did away with the necessity of discovering a road from Nursling to Bitterne. I therefore took it for granted that the road described by Leman and Hatcher in the New Forest was the continuation of the Winchester-Nursling road. Having thus cleared the ground, I again consulted the MS. edition of the old one-inch Ordnance Map at

---

to the existence of remains of such a road at Boyatt Farm and at other points farther south.

[1] *The History of Modern Wiltshire*, by Sir R. C. Hoare; *Old and New Sarum or Salisbury*, by Robert Benson and Henry Hatcher, London, John Nichols, 1843, p. 4.

Southampton, and, sure enough, I found a causeway marked as running across a common east of Barrow Hill, Copythorne. I copied the entry on to my map, and on visiting the spot had no difficulty in finding it; in places it is in a state of perfect preservation. The two ends of this fragment I also succeeded in prolonging—the eastern end as far as a point about half a mile due north of Tachbury earthwork, the western end to Stony Cross.

The westward extension of this fragment between Copythorne and Stony Cross presents many features which are instructive in the tracing of Roman roads. In one place the road crossed a low flat piece of ground which had not been under plough for very long.[1] The soil was black and peaty; and the road showed up most clearly as a broad raised mound of yellow gravel. Farther on it ascends the rising ground towards Malwood, and in one place the causeway crosses a gully and has dammed up a streamlet, forming a small marshy pond. I had observed the same occurrence in the case of the Lepe road; and now determined to add it to the list of clues to be used in building up hypotheses.

While trying to find traces of this road on Fritham Common, I accidentally discovered a new and hitherto unsuspected Roman road. I was walking from the Bell Inn at Brook, my headquarters, to the common on the southern edge of Fritham enclosure, and as I came up out of the

[1] It is shown as rough common on the map of 1806-8.

forest on to the open plateau I observed a dark line in the heather which looked like the flattened causeway of a Roman road. I went and inspected it, found it satisfactory, and traced it into the enclosures of Fritham northwards, and to the south as far as Minstead Manor. But beyond these points it has defied my utmost endeavours to trace it. This is the only case where I have discovered a Roman road entirely by accident. It is instructive, for it shows the value of keeping a sharp lookout whenever one is working in the field. Afterwards I found that the indefatigable Leman, or rather his friend Crocker, had been before me, but the description they gave did not enable me to find any trace of the road on the ground where they described its course, and where I had already failed to find it. The road in question is clearly making for Old Sarum, and southwards it may possibly be a continuation of the Lepe road. It is, however, more likely that it went to Lymington.

A road which had often puzzled me was that from Spinae, north-westward along the Wickham-Stockcross ridge, separating the Kennet and Lambourne valleys. As far southwards as Wickham it was quite clear and followed the modern Baydon road, but beyond that point it was uncertain. It had always been assumed that the Roman road coincided with the modern Newbury road, which runs in straight sections for most of the way. It does not, however, run quite straight, nor does there appear to be any valid reason for the alterations in its course. The country must have been fairly open in Roman times, especially on the flat top of the ridge, and if it followed this it would certainly have kept a straight course. Nowhere are there any vestiges of a causeway, either at the side of or underneath the modern road, nor has excavation at specially selected points by its side revealed any signs of such. I therefore decided to throw overboard the accepted view and to start afresh. I remembered the existence of an ancient pond called Sole Pond, at the head of a valley running into the Lambourne. This pond is formed by a dam thrown across the valley, which dam is now used by a cart-track. It occurred to me that this pond might have had the same origin as those which I found in the New Forest and which there were caused by the damming action of the gravel causeway of Roman roads. I therefore visited the spot in company with my friend Mr. Harold Peake, of Boxford, who knew the neighbourhood thoroughly. We examined the pond and found distinct traces of a continuation of the causeway south-eastwards and unmistakable signs of it in a field immediately south-east of the road from Boxford to Hoe Benham, just west of Upper Farm. Beyond that point we traced it over hill and dale for two miles, as far as Stockcross Station. North-westwards we found signs of it in Sole Common wood accompanied by deeply-cut hollow pack-trails.

These old overgrown hollow-trails or 'hollow-ways' are almost invariably found by the side of

Roman roads when they climb hills, and they were probably caused by the traffic which followed the course of the Roman road, both contemporary with and subsequent to it. In many cases they are clearly of later date, and often, as here, they have partially destroyed the remains of the causeway itself. They probably began to be deeply cut when the Romans were evacuating Britain and were therefore unable to keep their roads in good repair. Then, again, the traffic which had learnt to follow the line of the road from one settlement to another would not keep on the crown of the causeway, but yet would not wander far enough from it to lose its help as a guide to the direction in which it was proceeding. Also it should be remembered that the road itself was probably less useful than the clearing of forest and scrub which had to take place when it was constructed. The soft grass and heather by its side would be more pleasant going for horse and mule traffic than the hard road, except across marshy country. Hence the whole of the cleared area, which must have been a little wider everywhere than the road itself, would be used. In the Sudan at the present day similar long straight clearings have been made through the thorny impenetrable scrub for the purpose of erecting a line of telegraph poles. The track thus cleared has naturally become a highway for all traffic on camels and donkeys and on foot, though the primary purpose was to erect the telegraph poles.

The above instance is instructive in two ways.

It shows the failure of one hypothesis when tested in the field both by observation and excavation; and the success of another, based upon previously observed facts. Moreover an examination of the map and the ruling of a pencil-line showed that the prolongation of the road south-eastwards from the place of its last undoubted occurrence brought it some way to the north-east of the top of the ridge, on its lower slopes, very close to Sole Pond. This fact, which I discovered after I had begun to suspect Sole Pond, was very suggestive. It proved the value of a rule which I invariably observe whenever I lose track of a Roman road — to go back and start again at the point where it was last seen on the ground and where its existence was proved beyond question. The observance of this rule has saved me much aimless wandering and has put me on the right track many a time. It is astonishing how often one picks up the right course again quite easily through noting some indication previously overlooked. Moreover there are often two alternative possibilities and one may select the wrong one first time. It is not only in the field that this rule applies. It is equally applicable indoors, especially when one is smoking the final pipe after a day's hunting, with a map of the country in front of one. It is then that the results of the day's work begin to fall into their true perspective. Then is the time, if one has lost the scent, to say honestly to oneself, ' Where did I last see it beyond a doubt ? ' The answer must be frankly made, even if it washes out the whole day's work. The day will not have been wasted; for it will at least have produced a negative result. Stern self-criticism is the surest way to ultimate success. Having gone back, on the map this time, to the last certain point, it will usually be possible to form some hypothesis to test next day. By the building up and testing of hypotheses we steadily advance, and the facts available for use as evidence next time increase in number with each discovery.

The last instance I shall take is that of the Silchester-Speen road. The existence of this road was postulated by the Antonine Itineraries, but nothing certain was known of any single portion of its course. It had been observed that a modern road ran almost—but yet not quite—straight out of the west gate of the Roman town of Silchester for a distance of about a mile as far as a boulder of sarsen stone known as the Impstone. Upon no evidence whatever worth the name this stone was supposed to be an ancient Roman milestone, and the name 'Imp'-Stone to be derived from a non-existent inscription on it containing the abbreviation IMP (for Imperator). The coincidence of the road with a county boundary lent force to the argument in its favour, but the coincidence is only partial as the road ceases farther west where the parish and county boundary bends slightly northwards. I had long provisionally adopted this hypothesis as being the only one current, and I searched Greenham and Crookham Commons from end to end in search of a continuation of it there. These two commons, which are really one large tract of barren heath land, occupy a plateau dividing the Kennet and Enbourne Valleys. It has never been under plough in any part, with the possible exception of the eastern portion, and if the Roman road ever crossed it some remains *must* have survived. I failed absolutely to discover any, though I made a most exhaustive search over every portion. This method of elimination was necessary when hypotheses failed one after the other—all based on the assumption that the Impstone portion was authentic. Moreover the existence of a large tract of undisturbed waste land right across the path it should have followed made the search less arduous and more promising than otherwise. It also greatly enhanced the value of the negative evidence it provided in the result. When, therefore, I had searched every part in vain I decided to abandon the idea that the Impstone road could be the Roman road, and began to look about for an alternative course. I was put on the right track by a footnote in Samuel Barfield's *History of Thatcham*,[1] where the author stated his belief that the road ran ' through Aldermaston Soke and Park, Harbour Hill, Wasing Park, Shalford . . .'. Examining the six-inch map in the light of this account, I observed a diagonal hedge-line just north-west of

[1] Vol. i., 1901, p. 14. The reference given there to Gough Additional MS. 4to. 1, in the Bodleian Library, is merely to a copy of *Archaeologia*, xv., 1806, pp. 179-191, where Dr. Beeke recorded some observations in this neighbourhood.

Silchester Walls, which was roughly in alignment with the fence of a pine wood farther on and also with a portion of the modern road where it crosses a valley at Aldermaston Soke. Things began to look very promising, and I determined to examine it at the first opportunity. I found the causeway very well preserved on the edge of the wood and traceable right on to the gate of Silchester : while westwards I followed it without a break across the Kennet Valley to the modern village of Thatcham.[1] Later I was able to prove its existence on the marshy floor of the Kennet Valley by cutting a trench through a well-preserved portion near Brimpton Mill.

Several interesting points emerge from the discovery of this road. In the first place, it shows the value of examining the ancient and often discarded theories of older archaeologists.[2] A great deal that they wrote is useless to us, and consists merely of vague speculation. Some few of them, however, took pleasure in riding on horseback about the wild heath-covered tracts and over the breezy chalk downs, examining ancient roads and earth-

[1] I cannot at the moment lay my hand on the earliest mention of this north-westerly course through Aldermaston Soke; but I believe it was started as a hypothesis during the eighteenth century by Dr. Beeke or another of the same school of antiquaries. At any rate their writings contain many references to Roman roads in this locality which have been very useful.

[2] Barfield's later course is along ' Crookham Manor Lane, passing to the south side of Chamberhouse Manor Farm ; then by Bowdown, Greenham fields, through Newbury (crossing the Kennet near the Church), and so on to Speen Hill'. I followed this course until I failed anywhere along it to find satisfactory evidence of the road. Returning to the last certain point I soon picked up the right trail.

works and putting their observations on record. Unfortunately the record itself is often hidden away in a mass of irrelevant matter which has prejudiced later investigators against them, and caused the whole to be written off as worthless without discriminating between chaff and grain. But it should be remembered that these old fellows had opportunities which are denied to us, for they lived in the days before the Enclosure Acts, when much larger tracts of waste land existed, happy hunting-grounds for the field archaeologist. True, their means of locomotion were confined to the horse and to Shanks's pony, but both are less exacting than the bicycle, which is a fastidious animal and no true friend of the field archaeologist of to-day, whose way lies across country and away from metalled roads.

It is, therefore, always desirable that, in addition to forming new theories of one's own, recourse should be had to any existing theories that seem promising. They *may* rest upon a basis of observed facts. In any case it is always advisable to test them on the ground, if only to reject them. Sometimes, as in this case, they will put one on the right track, and save one a great deal of time and unprofitable labour—unprofitable, that is, in so far as it leads one no further on the particular line of inquiry that is being followed. But it is very rarely that a day in the field can be written down as wholly devoid of positive results. When looking for this very road in the part where Barfield goes astray I discovered the remains of the ancient moated manor of Crookham, indicated only on the map by the names 'Upper Ash Moat' and 'Lower Ash Moat', applied to two curious elongated strips of undergrowth.[1] But while it is always good to keep one's eyes open, and to note and record, *on the spot*, on the six-inch map everything that one sees of interest, it is best to concentrate one's purpose on one object at a time.

Another point which is brought out by the discovery of this road is the importance of watching for 'unnatural' hedge-lines, especially those which run diagonally across the country and which are approximately straight for any considerable distance. The usual shape of an enclosed field is a rectangle or square, and the resulting pattern on the six-inch map is a network of such rectangles, or, more accurately, four-sided figures. Any deviation should be looked upon with suspicion. The field archaeologist will soon learn to distinguish, even on the map, the mathematically straight line of a wooden fence from the uncertain, wavy, but yet approximately straight line of an old-established hedge on a Roman road. Such hedges often followed the course of the ancient Roman causeway which provided the farmer with a convenient boundary. It was the alignment of two such boundaries (of woods in this case) which first suggested to Mr. Peake

---

[1] This discovery proved very valuable later in identifying the Saxon bounds of the parish of Brimpton. See *The Antiquary*, July 1915.

the course of the Roman road from Speen to Marlborough, near Leverton cross-roads.[1]

In this instance also I was helped by the existence of parallel pack-trails by the side of the road, where it follows the edge of Callow Wood. In places the road itself is obliterated by them, as is the case with the Cirencester-Speen road near Sole Pond. Such trails may be used as guides to the course of the road where it is doubtful, but they must be used with extreme caution, and should never be used as evidence without some facts in very strong support elsewhere in its course. They may then be used to bridge a gap. If we know for certain that a road existed at points A and C, then we may restore its course over the missing portion B from the evidence of trails. The reason that they must be used so cautiously is of course that they went on being formed right up to the introduction of metalled roads, and indeed are still forming in large tracts of open country like the New Forest.

The field archaeologist will learn more from actual experience than from any amount of advice given by another. But it may be helpful to give him the results of another's experience; he will at any rate get some idea as to the sort of evidence with which he has to deal.

First and foremost, he should never set out for a day's work without a six-inch map of the area he

---

[1] See *Berks, Bucks and Oxon Archaeological Journal*, vol. xiii. (October 1907) pp. 82-86, ' Romano-British Berkshire '.

proposes to examine. The one-inch map is on too small a scale for entries to be recorded on it. Each six-inch sheet encloses an area of two miles by three, costs one shilling and sixpence, and can be obtained by return of post on application to the Director-General, Ordnance Survey Office, Southampton, enclosing a postal order and a maximum amount of 4d. for postage and packing. It is advisable also to buy an index-sheet of the six-inch sheets, published by counties, price 2d. a county. He should have by him a copy of the one-inch sheet of the area upon which to enter his final results in pencil. Entered thus, day by day, the mutual relationship of detached fragments and their possible connection is more apparent, and will provide food for thought and hypotheses after the day's work.

The actual plotting of the course of a road is easy. Measurements can be made by pacing along a hedge or road from the nearest junction; often they can be estimated by eye. When the road goes through a wood it is more difficult to plot it, but unless the wood is a very large one, or unless the road is suspected of altering its direction during its passage through it, it will be enough to measure and mark in the points where it enters and leaves the wood. If the wood is a large one there are sure to be paths or drives cut through it which it must cross. It will then be necessary to walk up each path, counting one's steps until the road is reached. The distance paced can then be plotted on the map with the aid of a piece of paper, or, better, a visiting card, and the scale at the bottom of the sheet. I find it convenient to carry a visiting-card with a scale of feet already marked off in ink upon it. If the distance is long the hundreds can be kept on the fingers of one's hand. The business of finding the road at all in a wood is difficult, especially when there is thick undergrowth. Hence an opportunity should be watched for when the undergrowth is cut down, a periodical event in all well-kept woods. Winter and early spring are the best seasons for work; for then the leaves are off the trees, and the ground everywhere can be seen much better.

In pacing distances the natural pace should be used, at any rate for long distances. Therefore its length should be ascertained by pacing alongside a tape, or over a measured distance of not less than thirty yards. The exact coefficient can easily be worked out for turning paces into feet or yards. The back of a six-inch map is useful for such calculations, as well as for other notes which cannot go on the other side. The margin of the map, however, is the best place for these notes when there is room for them, with a line and arrow to indicate the place referred to.

It would be advisable — though I confess I have not done so consistently hitherto—to adopt some definite system of classification, based on the nature of the evidence for the existence of a road. At the one extreme, direct and positive evidence consisting of visible remains of a causeway; at the other, we have complete absence of such evidence, but only an *a priori* probability that it existed. I suggest solid double line for the former, and open broken lines for the latter. For all intermediate kinds of evidence an open double line may be used: ▬▬ ═══ ┈┈┈┈

In tracing these roads it is generally safe to assume that the sectors were laid out in a dead straight line between the turning-points. All the more important, therefore, is it to determine the exact position of these turning-points. For reasons already stated they usually occur on hill-tops or on the brow of valley-sides. It is often a great help to notice the position of prominent trees, gaps in a wood or hedge, etc., which are situated on the road, and to align these behind one as one advances. Of course a pencil-line ruled upon the map will serve the same purpose, but it is less handy, and, moreover, one learns something of the way in which the road was originally laid out by adopting the visual method. A tall Douglas fir, which stands on the top of a hill at Chilworth Court near Southampton, grows right on the actual causeway of the Winchester-Nursling road, and it was a great help to me in following it: for it forms a landmark for the whole neighbourhood.˙ While standing on a hill from which an uninterrupted view can be obtained, it is a good thing to carry the eye (as far as one can) in the direction followed by the road. The limit of sight will probably be the hill-top where the next alteration of its course will occur. In doing so the map [1] should be consulted, and allowance should be made for alteration in vegetation since Roman times. Where there is now an unobstructed view may have then been dense forest, and where there are now plantations the ground may have been open heath.

The actual means by which a Roman road may be detected are legion. They vary with the character of the materials of which it was made, and with differences at the present day in the soil and state of cultivation of the country traversed. In a chalk country the roads were made on a foundation of large, unhewn flints quarried from the upper chalk. If all traces of a raised causeway have been ploughed away, its course may sometimes be indicated by a preponderance of large, rough flints in a certain part of the field, forming a wide belt across it. They represent the causeway in its last stage of decay. Very often they will be preserved in the bank of a hedge, especially if the hedge be an old one. When the field has been sown with corn, it will often be noticed that the course of the road is marked by a belt of sparse growth or a string of bare patches, due to the stony nature of the soil where the road once existed. Similarly in land under grass the course of the road may be indicated by the brown colour of the grass, especially in late summer or autumn and after dry seasons. It is therefore always advisable to visit suspected

[1] The half-inch layered map is best for this.

places at different seasons of the year. What is invisible during one season may be strikingly apparent during another. Sometimes a clue may be obtained from a gap in a hedge or fence. This may be due as before to the stony nature of the soil which retards the growth of the hedge in that part. A gap in an artificial wooden fence or paling may be a guide, especially when it runs along the top of a bank. It is then due to the greater loosening of the soil of the bank at this point, which here consists of loose stony rubble from the causeway, without the usual intermixture of binding loam.

In passing I would remark that all these minor points have actually been observed in tracing Roman roads in places where there is clear collateral evidence of the causeway : they have never been used singly as evidence without other support. It is questionable how far such minor points should be used as direct evidence in the present state of our knowledge. Perhaps when more workers join in the search we shall be better able to assess their value. At present such points are better used as guides than as evidence, and they always require careful handling. In any case no harm will be done by using them as guides if their use as such is clearly indicated on the map and in the published account.

Whenever a road is cut through by a chalk- or clay-pit or stone quarry the sides should be carefully examined for signs of the road. When a good exposure occurs, careful measurements should be made (a notched walking-stick will do), both horizontal and vertical, and a section drawn to scale. Neither measurements nor drawing need much expert surveying skill. Good exposed sections are rare, but help to identification may often be obtained from the sides of a pond or from a freshly-cleaned drainage ditch. In one instance [1] I was able, by taking 'soundings' with my walking-stick along the bottom of such a ditch, to feel the rounded hump of the causeway right across its whole width. On the outer edges the stick could be pressed through the soft loam for some distance before encountering the stony layer. As I approached nearer to the crest the stick passed through less and less loam each time, until on the crest itself it refused to be driven in at all. There were hardly any signs of a *raised* causeway visible, because it had become buried by the accumulation of loam. In ploughed fields the *deep* furrow should always be carefully examined and prodded.

Often the only evidence is an admixture of sandy grit in the soil. This is, I imagine, the remains of the outer surface of the road and the rain-washings from it. It is the same fine grit that we get on our modern flint roads. Of course this evidence will not probably be available outside a tertiary or chalk district, where the worn surface tends to form a powder and so become dissolved or blown away. But, throughout, I am speaking of Roman roads in the south and east of England, where they are generally made of flint.

[1] On the Silchester-Speen road east of Shalford Farm.

ROMAN ROADS

Sometimes a cottage, cowshed or hay-stack will give a clue, especially in marshy country, where advantage has been taken of the firm foundation provided by the causeway. Such a clue is valuable when forming a hypothesis with the aid of the map.

In one or two places near Southampton and also near Badbury Rings the road or causeway appears partly to have been made of rounded beach pebbles derived from a neighbouring outcrop of Tertiary strata. When these pebbles have been used over ground where they do not occur naturally—and their distribution is very restricted—they are valuable as evidence, even if the mound of the causeway has vanished. Other similar peculiarities are useful. I remember once seeing an exceptionally well-preserved fragment of a causeway just before it suddenly became lost.[1] It stopped abruptly at a fence separating a ploughed field from one which had never been under plough. In this case it was absolutely certain that the road once continued into the ploughed field, and the exact course it must have taken could be seen from high ground near-by. Yet all trace of the hump of the causeway had vanished, and the only evidence of its former existence was a greater preponderance of white flints, forming a belt across the field. This belt might have been entirely overlooked, or its evidence discounted under less favourable circumstances.

A word must be said as to evidence which is

[1] At Titlark Farm, near Chandlersford, Hampshire. See Williams-Freeman, *Field Archaeology*, p. 438.

unreliable. From the existence of a Roman villa it does not necessarily follow that a Roman highway passed near-by. These villas were generally, in Wessex, country farms, with no more relation to the artificial lines of the roads than have modern farms to a railway line. Nor can the finds of coins be used to postulate the existence of a Roman road. They are too commonly distributed to be of any value for this purpose. The discovery of primitive settlements, on the other hand, especially at points where the roads are suspected of crossing valleys, may be used to support other evidence that the road crossed at that point. The settlement in such circumstances is the direct result of the road, and has grown up from the traffic along it. Such settlements always tend to spring up at a crucial point in the course of a road.

CHAPTER XVI

ROMAN ROADS: DOCUMENTARY EVIDENCE

THE evidence upon which we rely for tracing the course of Roman roads is of two kinds, archaeological and documentary, as will probably have been gathered from the preceding chapter. The documentary evidence falls into two distinct classes. In the first class are the Itineraries of Antonine and the map of the Ravenna geographer; in the second is included all other documentary evidence whatsoever, both ancient maps and manuscripts. For practical purposes the map of the Ravenna geographer may be left out of account in the study of Roman roads in Britain; for the only British portion of it which survives is the eastern part of Kent and a fragment of E. Anglia. The map is a thirteenth-century copy of the original, and was made on a roll discovered in 1547 in the library of Conrad Peutinger of Augsburg. The original map was probably drawn about the year A.D. 650. Most unfortunately for us, that part of it which showed Great Britain was at the end of the roll.[1]

[1] This recalls the Roman poet's words, ' ultimus orbe Britannus ', the popular Roman conception of Britain being that it was ' the last place on earth '.

The Antonine Itineraries are much more useful. They consist of a list of the Roman stations of Britain, with the distances between them in Roman miles. The arrangement is that of a series of itineraries or route-marches, passing from one important centre to another, through less important ones. It is easy to criticise the accuracy of the itineraries, but my impression is that they are more reliable than is generally supposed. It is difficult, however, to use them at all adequately, in the absence of an up-to-date and scholarly critical edition of the manuscripts. Such a work is badly needed, and would constitute a suitable subject for university research.

The Itineraries of Antonine are the only direct documentary evidence for the course of Roman roads, and are often the only evidence which exists of the names of Roman towns and stations. Stray fragments of obscure Latin and Greek authors [1] often mention the names of British tribes, but never give much help towards locating their exact position. The first real assistance is given by the Anglo-Saxon boundaries of land which are placed at the end of charters recording gifts of land to monasteries or thegns.[2] These boundaries often mention Roman roads. They are not usually valuable in recovering the course of lost fragments

[1] See *History of the Ancient Britons*, by the Rev. J. A. Giles, 1847, vol. ii. Appendix of Original Documents : a most valuable collection, pirated from the less accessible *Vetusta Monumenta*.
[2] Collected together in W. de Grey Birch's *Cartularium Saxonicum* (3 vols.) and J. M. Kemble's *Codex Diplomaticus* (6 vols.).

so much as in confirming the existence of those which are supported only by archaeological evidence. Such confirmation is not of course essential if the archaeological evidence itself is conclusive, but it is useful in strengthening the faith of the weaker brethren. An instance of this occurred in the bounds of Brimpton (*Cart. Sax.* ii. 802) of which I published an account in *The Antiquary* for July 1915. At a certain point the bounds strike the Kennet Valley, where a ' Welshman's Bridge ' is mentioned (*weala brycge*). Now this spot can be identified exactly with the point now known as Quaking Bridge, which lies right on the course of the Roman road from Silchester to Speen. The causeway can actually be followed past the spot to-day; close by I dug a trench through a very well-preserved portion. Now the term ' Weala ' was used by the Saxons to denote things of Roman origin and construction, as I showed in that paper: it meant ' foreign ' and was used indiscriminately of all non-Saxon persons and things (just as every white man was called ' Turk ' by the adherents of the Mahdi). Hence the Saxon bounds provide a valuable confirmation of a road which had been discovered by archaeological field work and excavation.

The word used to denote a Roman road in Anglo-Saxon bounds is almost invariably ' street '. Whenever this term is used, a Roman road should be looked out for. Other words for roads are ' herepath ', ' weg ', ' paeð ', and ' anstigo '. ' Herepath' usually denotes an important highway of non-Roman origin; other roads or tracks were called 'weg'. 'Paeðs', and 'anstigs' are mere footpaths or bridleways.

All mediaeval documents which mention placenames or field-names, or which give the bounds of land should be searched for passages which may throw light on roads. The help given will probably be indirect, and often through the medium of the Saxon bounds. The chief reason for searching ancient deeds is for the help they give in identifying the Saxon charters, for they often contain placenames which occur also in the charters but have since dropped out. Or they may provide an explanatory link in the chain of the evolution from Saxon times to the present day. During this period names sometimes change almost out of recognition. These land-documents are also a valuable aid to the identification of Forest Perambulations, which in their turn sometimes throw light on Roman roads and the charters.

When we come to later times we get help from Tithe Maps and Enclosure Award Maps and their attached terriers. Here, again, the help is not often direct, but more often consists in the general contribution which these documents make to one's knowledge of the evolution of the topography of a district. Let me take an imaginary case to illustrate this. Suppose you are tracing a Roman road across fields, and are in doubt as to whether a broad, stony bank, much flattened and ploughed over, represents the causeway or not. A reference to the Tithe Map, or, better, the Award Map of the parish (if available), may show that a hedge-line formerly ran along this bank. Now it is of course not impossible that this old hedge-line marked the course of the Roman road ; but it is clear that in this case the bank has no necessary connection with a Roman causeway, but represents merely the remains of an ancient balk or field-boundary. For there is always a tendency for stones to accumulate on the edge of a field, especially on a slope, and the field-archaeologist should always be on the look-out for such ploughed-out boundaries. Very often it is extremely difficult to determine simply from inspection in the field whether a given bank [1] of this nature is a ploughed-out boundary or the remains of a causeway.

All old maps are valuable for the light they throw on Roman roads. Reference has already been made to the old edition of the one-inch O.S. map and to the original manuscript sheets (1800–1830) preserved at Southampton. In addition, the maps compiled by private enterprise should be consulted, such as Isaac Taylor's *Hampshire* (1759) and *Dorset* (1765), Rocque's *Berks* (1761) and Andrews and Duruy's *Wilts* (1773), and those of Sir Richard Colt Hoare, published in his *Ancient Wilts* (1812, 1819). Some of these maps were made

---

[1] ' Bank ' is a bad word for such. ' Mound ' is better but usually connotes ' round ' as well, whereas these ' mounds ' are, of course, long raised belts.

by persons who had an enlightened interest in ancient remains. Sir Richard Colt Hoare's were the result of a special survey made by Mr. Crocker, whom Sir Richard employed privately; their object was therefore primarily archaeological. As both Sir Richard and his surveyor had a keen eye for field-archaeology, their maps are invaluable, and they are, perhaps, still the best archaeological maps which have ever been made of Wessex. Isaac Taylor, though less directly concerned with archaeology, did not lose sight of ancient roads and earthworks in making his map.

The help of the old maps on a smaller scale is often indirect. For instance, the descriptions which were given by eighteenth-century antiquaries of the course followed by a road often contain references to obsolete names of houses, cross-roads, etc., which it is difficult to identify on the modern Ordnance Map. But if the contemporary maps (which they probably had before them in writing the account) are consulted, the difficulties vanish. Such is the case with the road running north out of Silchester towards Streatley. The description of Mr. Beke contains several references to names which it would be difficult to identify without a map like that given in Robertson's road book.

Between 1830 and 1840 the authorities of the Staff College at Sandhurst suddenly took an interest in Roman roads. The cadets were made to follow their course and subsequently to construct a kind of route-traverse of them. Written accounts were

ROMAN ROADS

published in the Journal of the United Services Institution, but no trace of the maps can be found now at the Staff College,[1] the War Office, the Royal United Services Institution or the British Museum. This is the more regrettable as one of them, of the Silchester-Hungerford road, is said to have been seven feet long and to have ' constituted a superb specimen of topographical drawing ',[2] at a time when that art was at its zenith. Its scale must have been about 4″ to the mile.

Stored away in the libraries of county archaeological societies there are often to be found books of manuscript notes, made by antiquaries in the eighteenth and early nineteenth centuries. Such notes sometimes contain a grain of recorded observation buried in bushels of speculative chaff. They have therefore to be searched. It is dreary work, but seldom wholly unprofitable, even if the only result be the insight one gets into the attitude of mind of the author to his subject. Sometimes, too, one finds plums which fully repay one for one's trouble. Such was my discovery in the Library of the Wiltshire Archaeological Society at Devizes of a manuscript book of notes made by the Rev.

[1] With the exception of ' one executed in 1838, of the country lying immediately to the east of Bath, which extends eastwards only to the neighbourhood of Chippenham'. (Letter to the author from General Kiggell, Commandant of the Staff College, Camberley, dated July 6, 1914.)

[2] *United Services Journal*, Dec. 1836 (Part 3, p. 567). This map was exhibited at the Royal Military College, Sandhurst, in November 1836, with another, on a scale of one inch to the mile, ' which had been reduced from the great survey of the country between Staines and Silchester'. The latter is in the British Museum.

Thomas Leman. This book was bequeathed by him at his death in 1826 to Sir R. C. Hoare with whose collections it passed into the hands of the Wiltshire Society. His notes, though made over a century ago, are of the first rank in importance.

Leman was born at Kirkstead, in Norfolk, in 1751. At Cambridge he formed a friendship with William Bennet, who as Bishop of Cloyne afterwards conferred upon him the Chancellorship of Cloyne — which Leman was obliged to resign in 1802 on account of non-residence! Along with Archdeacon Coxe he assisted Sir Richard Colt Hoare in planning the *History of Ancient Wiltshire*.[1] Thirteen volumes of notes he bequeathed to the Bath Institution, where they are now kept. For the most part they consist of genealogical notes, but amongst them is a volume of Cary's *Atlas of England and Wales*, with Leman's ideas as to ancient and Roman roads marked in. He was fond of riding and had a passion for following Roman roads. He was well connected, and whenever staying at a country-seat he would take the opportunity of exploring the district on horseback, entering the results in his note-book in elegant, spidery writing. These notes were occasionally illustrated by diagrams, and often contained observations on discoveries of archaeological import not belonging to the Roman period. In many ways Leman deserves to rank among our greatest archaeo-

[1] *Dictionary of National Biography.*

logists. He had the true scientific spirit; realising the unity of all knowledge, past, present and future, he records, for the benefit of posterity, facts which did not interest his own generation. 'Having passed my summer of 1797 at Southampton', he says, 'I shall now endeavour to set down such particular antiquities as I think are unobserved by others, and which may probably one day tend to elucidate the obscure local history of this part of England.' It has taken over a hundred years for these words to come true; all the more honour, then, to the man who wrote them, for he was a hundred years before his time. He was one of the first field-archaeologists.

In addition to his own observations Leman recorded those of others, some of them personal friends of his own. Amongst the most valuable are those of Crocker. This man had a keen eye for old roads, but as far as I know he never published anything himself. Leman's accounts appear to have been derived from personal intercourse and correspondence with him. While showing much critical and discriminating insight—rare virtues in his age—he often quotes several mutually inconsistent accounts of the course followed by a road. It is, however, quite right to do so where doubt exists as to the course.

I hope some day to find time to publish a full critical edition of this note-book. It is a piece of work that is well worth doing, but must be lengthy if carried out in a manner worthy of the care originally bestowed upon it. Incidentally, the notes throw light on the difficulties of the field archaeologist at that time, before the Ordnance Maps were available.[1]

Much help in the tracing of Roman roads may be obtained from a study of parish boundaries. These boundaries have often remained unaltered since Saxon times, when, of course, the Roman roads were much better known and preserved than they are to-day. The existence of a straight portion of parish boundary often gives a clue, especially if it is in alignment with another straight portion or a modern road. When a modern road, which is suspected of occupying the site of a Roman road, is also followed by a parish boundary, the presumption in favour of the identification is greatly strengthened. On the other hand, it must be observed that many ancient and probably pre-Roman roads are followed by parish boundaries; often they form the frontier of two groups of parishes. There is, however, little difficulty in distinguishing roads of this class from Roman roads.

The examples quoted above in illustration of methods have all been taken from the south of England, and from that part of it which is known as Wessex. That is because it is the region with which I am most familiar. In the study of Roman roads, as in all archaeological work, it is advisable

---

[1] I have to thank the Rev. E. H. Goddard, Hon. Librarian of the Wiltshire Archaeological Society, for facilities in examining the book.

to confine one's attention to a certain region, and to deal with it exhaustively. For the Roman period my area is a four-sided figure, bounded on the south by the sea, and whose four corners are Dorchester (Dorset), Bath, Silchester and Chichester.[1] The actual area includes a certain periphery round each of these towns (as well as a marginal strip to the north of the northern frontier-line) retained to show their geographical environment, and to enable the sheet-lines of the map to be drawn straight. I propose some day to publish the results on a scale of a quarter of an inch to the mile, on a map showing modern features in grey. The Roman roads will be shown in red; so will Roman towns and stations (with names where possible), villas and potteries. Little else will be shown. The accompanying letterpress will be merely an explanation of the map, and of the large scale plans (mostly 2" or 3" to the mile) which accompany it. The course of each road will be described and the reasons for locating it; also a history will be given of various theories held about it in the past by archaeologists or antiquaries.

It will be obvious that similar methods are applicable to the rest of England, and especially to the regions west and east of the Wessex region. It is highly desirable that some one should undertake these two regions: he will not regret it when once he has started—indeed he will find it very

[1] It may be necessary to enlarge this area so as to include Somersetshire and Southern Gloucestershire.

hard to desist, unless I am much mistaken. He should, whenever possible, dig a trench through well-preserved portions of the roads, in order to establish some general principles regarding their dimensions and construction. He should verify doubtful portions by the same means. He should also dig trenches where no remains at all are visible on the surface, having previously chosen the exact spot by careful alignments with a pencil and ruler on the six-inch map. The trench may have to be rather a long one, but what of that in these days of communication-trenches miles in length? If the road passed that way, he can hardly fail to find some signs of it. If the soil is chalk he will be certain to find it or the drainage-ditches by its side : for we know now from experience that when once chalk has been disturbed by man the marks can never be obliterated. Trench-work of this kind is easy and rapid, and the results repay the slight trouble a hundredfold. When trenching cannot be undertaken even surface measurements are valuable, if a sectional drawing is made from them. They are best done with a spirit-level and staff, but quite good results are possible with very simple tools. I would refer those who wish to learn how to take these measurements to Dr. Williams-Freeman's book, *Field Archaeology as illustrated by Hampshire*, which should be in every one's library. The illustrations in that work are sufficient proof of the value of such measurements and of the excellent results that can be obtained with a walking-stick and bamboo rods. It is a game that needs two to play, but only one need be an expert.

Of the pleasures and fascination of field-work I shall say little. Those who have experienced them do not need to be told, and those who have not will only realise them when they have tried them. There is no sport so thrilling as the tracking of a Roman road across country. Moreover, it is a valuable offset to work in the study. There comes a time when the archaeologist gets stale from overmuch poring indoors over maps and books, and his work loses freshness and vitality. Then is the time to go off and do a spell of field-work. He will return home with many new discoveries and much food for reflection. He will take up his work again with renewed zest, and the work itself will be inspired by memories of the days spent on the open downs and commons.

CHAPTER XVII

EXCAVATION

' To suppose that excavating—one of the affairs which needs the widest knowledge—can be taken up by persons who are ignorant of most or all of the technical requirements, is a fatuity which has led, and still leads, to the most miserable catastrophes. Far better let things lie a few centuries longer under the ground, if they can be let alone, than repeat the vandalisms of past ages without the excuse of being a barbarian.'—W. M. Flinders-Petrie.

From what has gone before it might perhaps be thought that the archaeologist is mainly dependent upon surface observations and chance finds. That, however, is not so. He can acquire his own finds at any time by deliberate excavation, though I hasten to add that knowledge, not loot, should be the object of his labours. It will be obvious that a single object thus found and accurately recorded will tell him much more than if it were a casual find.[1]

The one essential feature in every excavation—apart from the presence and direction of an expert—is a plan of the site. That is realised by nearly all excavators nowadays, thanks to General Pitt-

---

[1] In the following paragraphs I have in mind excavation on a small scale in this country rather than on a large scale (as in the East).

Rivers. A plan of an ancient site corresponds in importance to an archaeological map of a large area. It is generally advisable to make the plan of a site some time before digging begins, for then one's whole attention is taken up with studying the soils and observing the *gisement* of finds. It is best to peg out the whole area to be excavated, and a little more, preferably into twenty-metre squares, and to rule out a similar system of squares on a sheet of drawing paper. The scale will vary, but 1/200 is a generally useful one. Next, if earthworks of any kind are involved, levels should be taken at frequent intervals (say every four metres) with a view to drawing contours. Sometimes, however, it is better to contour the site directly. In either case it is important to finish before the first sod is cut.

Having made a plan of the site, digging may begin. The number of men employed will vary according to the funds and time available. Personally, I very much prefer when excavating in England to employ a couple of workmen. Progress, of course, is slow, but it is very sure; and the work costs no more than employing more men for shorter time. The workman is like an 'extra-corporeal limb' of one's body, and one learns to feel the ground vicariously through the end of his prong. Thus one gains a far better insight into the soil-conditions, because one's attention is concentrated upon one thing at a time. All the advantages of digging with one's own hands are present, and none of the disadvantages. With more men concentration is difficult as they will probably be working in different parts of the site at the same time. But a two-men dig is an ideal not often attainable in practice. In general, the excavator's motto when he is working in ' pay-dirt ' should be ' more haste, less speed '.

I am not an advocate of digging ' trial trenches ' indiscriminately, without a set purpose. They may do more harm than good, especially if the results are not immediately followed up. But it is impossible to dogmatise. Trenches through the ditch and vallum of an earthwork are of course most valuable if carefully made and accompanied by accurate measurements. One ditch completely cleaned out, however, is more valuable than single trenches across the ditches of a dozen different earthworks. As a rule, trenching, if unavoidable, should be abandoned at the first possible moment. The aim of an excavator should be rather to remove or peel off the accumulation of debris from a site or a grave, and thus expose it to view as it appeared when abandoned by the original occupiers of the place. This is not always easy, but I have never found a soil where it was impossible. Here the local knowledge of local men is invaluable. The intending excavator should endeavour to obtain as a digger at least one intelligent navvy who has dug extensively in the neighbourhood, and who will thereby have acquired a sure eye in distinguishing natural soil from soil which has been disturbed.

EXCAVATION

Natural soil or bedrock—what the Egyptians call 'gebel'—is that which has never been moved by the hand of man. All else is artificial soil. When working with a really good navvy who knows his soils, the excavator has little to do at first but watch the navvy, his professor, at work; but, as in all good teaching, both teacher and learner merge into researchers. If the excavator has much previous experience (and if he has not he should be an assistant only), he will, of course, be at an advantage over the navvy who knows only the soils of a small district, and has hitherto regarded them from a slightly different point of view. But what the navvy does know he knows thoroughly well. Digging is his job, and he can feel with the prongs of his fork like an ant with its antennae. In this he has an advantage over the excavator, who relies mainly upon his eyes. But the latter should, however, frequently borrow a pick or fork and prod the ground with it, if only to improve his own knowledge.

Sometimes it is possible by clearing off the topsoil and one spit, and by scraping clean the area thus laid bare, to detect a difference in colour or hardness above certain spots. The difference in colour can be detected by the excavator, but not the difference in hardness. That should be discovered by the workman who has picked the ground over, and he should accordingly be warned beforehand to look out for such soft spots. They indicate holes or trenches which have been artificially excavated and then filled up again—slowly by nature

212   MAN AND HIS PAST

(in the case of ditches or pit-dwellings) or rapidly by man (in the case of graves). The next step is to remove the filling of soil, which will generally peel off quite easily from the undisturbed hard bedrock. The original shape of the hole or ditch will then be disclosed. If it be the ditch outside an earthwork, which, of course, has been filled up naturally through the action of frost, rain and wind, its

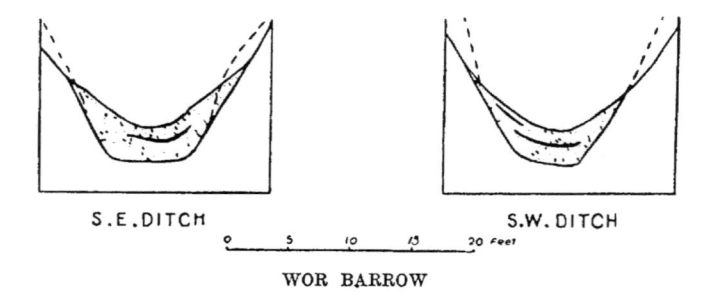

S.E.DITCH   S.W. DITCH
0   5   10   15   20 Feet
WOR BARROW

bottom will be covered by a fairly deep deposit of 'rapid silting' which has taken only a very few years to accumulate, and which will therefore be of the same age as the earthwork itself. It has been proved experimentally by General Pitt-Rivers that rapid silting will accumulate in four years to a depth of 2½ feet.[1] Any relics (especially pot-

[1] *Excavations in Cranborne Chase*, vol. iv., 1898, p. 24, Figs. reproduced above (Presidential Address to the Archaeological Institute of Great Britain and Ireland, Dorchester, August 3, 1897). The General re-excavated in 1897 the ditch of Wor Barrow (a Long Barrow) which he had previously excavated in 1893 and then left exposed to the action of natural agencies. He remarks: 'The investigation shows that all the fragments of pottery that had been found by me in the old chalk rubble were of the period of the first construction of the ditch, or within a year or two after it,

sherds, however rude) found lying on the bottom of the ditch or *in* the rapid silting are of the greatest value, for from their character the earthwork itself can be dated. Anything found *above* the rapid silting is of value only in so far as it proves the earthwork to be of earlier date than the object found. A single isolated sherd is not evidence, as it might have been lying on the surface when the earthwork was being constructed.

The method of peeling off the debris layer by layer has this great advantage, that it is certain at what depth the objects are found. It is impossible that they can have come from a greater depth than the spit which is in process of removal. For this reason, even when digging a section through the ditch and rampart of an earthwork, only one spit should be removed at a time.

But enough has been said, I think, to show that British excavation, like Egyptology, is a science and art in itself, and it is impossible here to do more than to suggest some of the methods that should be adopted. The prime necessity in an excavator is experience gained under a master of the art; without it he will do far more harm than good by digging. The enthusiastic amateur will probably ruin a site irreparably, and should be warned off—or, better, helped—by an expert.

Those who would learn more about how to dig

---

and it accounts for so little having been found in this part of the silting, which had accumulated very rapidly '.

The whole of this address is a most valuable contribution to the literature of excavation by one who was the founder of that science.

should study General Pitt-Rivers' four volumes on Cranborne Chase[1] and Professor Petrie's *Methods and Aims in Archaeology* (Macmillan, 1904), and should pay a visit to the Farnham (Dorset) and Taunton Museums.

[1] Since the above chapter was written I have had an opportunity of testing the General's method of discovering pits and ditches that have silted up completely by means of hammering the surface with a pick. It has proved astonishingly accurate.

CHAPTER XVIII

MUSEUMS

'The present system of museums is the most serious bar to the progress of archaeology.'—W. M. Flinders-Petrie.

ALL those who have any familiarity with English provincial museums will realise the truth of the words which stand at the head of this chapter. The word 'museum' is itself a byword for dulness, dust and general decrepitude. The very atmosphere reeks of decay, and the sight of a few skulls and stuffed birds completes the illusion of a charnel-house. Our local museums are too frequently the tombs of the dead past, and the wonder is that they attract any visitors at all. Whence comes this atmosphere of gloom, repellent even to those of whose goodwill there can be no question? Why is it that in sorrow they refrain from entering the dismal portals?

It is, I think, partly because museums are still allowed by some curators to remain a disorderly dumping-ground of useless rubbish; because they still cling, if unconsciously, to the obsolete idea that a museum should attract by a show of monstrosities, curios, war trophies or *exceptions*. But for this curators are not wholly to blame; for they are not always men capable of rising superior to the education they have suffered. The average educational course, primary, secondary or even university, has practically no points of contact with the contents of any museum (whether good or bad), and, when it has, the teacher too often fails to call attention to the fact. Nor, while our educational time-table remains as narrow and circumscribed as it still is, can the museum authorities do much to help the teacher. I would even go further and say that curators should, where history is concerned, deliberately boycott certain schoolmasters rather than give any support or encouragement to a radically bad system. There is a vicious circle which excludes the chance of improvement. The schoolmaster is fettered by the claims of examinations and by demands of 'practical' parents; museum curators are recruited from the ranks of his pupils; and unless they be men of exceptional ability the vast possibilities of a museum do not occur to them. So long as a good museum remains a voice crying in the wilderness, its good influence is bound to be inappreciable. For there are few who have sufficient leisure or originality to use a museum as an instrument of self-education. In short, museums both good and bad have no connection with the life and ideas generally current to-day. If bad, they speak a dead language; if good, a foreign one.

MUSEUMS

A change, however, is coming. The idea of Universal History is in the air; and to those who are in the habit of watching for straws to show the direction of the wind, it is abundantly clear that before long the story of man's place in nature and his secular conquest of her will be taught in every school—even perhaps in our ' great ' public schools! Then the good museum will come into its own, and there will be elsewhere a great revival and rattling of dry bones. For universal history without a museum of reference is *Hamlet* without the Prince of Denmark.

What, then, will the good museum be like? First and foremost it must be weather-proof and well-lit: specimens are useless if they are allowed to decay, or if they cannot be easily seen. Then it must be arranged upon a system which corresponds with the logical arrangement of the subject-matter. Apart from specialist museums the only logical arrangement is that of time and space. Let me for a moment be allowed to hitch my creaking wagon to a star and describe an ideal museum in some far-off Utopia of the future. Let me free myself also from the shackles of a too anthropocentric outlook, and range over the whole field of nature. My museum is to be called the World Museum, and it will be situated in America. It will be very large, greater in length than breadth. Its long axis will be Time, its broad axis Space. Time will begin with the formation of the Solar System, the different hypotheses (if one does not by then prevail) being shown by models, and illustrated by photographs of stellar systems in different stages of development. Then will come drawings of the younger planets of our system in the order suggested by the present state of their evolution. Next, the beginning of the earth will be shown by model globes coloured to indicate the distribution of land and sea during the successive geological epochs. But the features shown in them will besides be as full and detailed as the existing state of knowledge allows. Each globe will stand in the middle of a well-lit room, round which will stand cases of fossils of the period in question. Above will be drawings by an artist with powers of constructive imagination, showing the fossil creatures as they appeared when alive, against a background of re-created environment. Here and there will be a living descendant (when such is to be found) made as comfortable as circumstances permit (though at best the poor prisoner can be but a martyr in a good cause). At an early stage of the geological record the museum will broaden out into side-galleries or transepts, allotted to the different regions of the world. Perhaps there will be a central corridor down the middle in which man's ancestors in the direct line will be shown : for by then we shall have traced his pedigree in detail back to the primordial cell. (Perhaps, however, man will have become more humble by then, and be content to submit to the same treatment as his poorer relations in the animal kingdom.) When we come to the Jurassic Period giant reptiles will be rather a problem to the curator; but the men of our Utopia will move too freely in space to be frightened by eighty feet or so. Every form of life which has come down to us will find a place; for each, after all, is the representative of a vast constituency of vanished genera and species. Not every one will necessarily be exhibited; there will be cabinets of drawers for the student (perhaps above the same space but on another floor). Over the portal will be written in large letters the name of the period, and below that the region to which the room is devoted. Every specimen will of course be fully labelled.

In due course we shall come to the Tertiary Period and the dawn of man. Every bone of man's early ancestors will be exhibited — casts when actual specimens are not available. With each will be the implements made and used by the men of the time. In the same room will be of course, as before, the fossil remains of all contemporary species. In these later periods, when it becomes possible to study regions in more detail, globes will be largely supplemented by flat maps on a uniform scale and projection. As we come to the later prehistoric periods of the Stone Age and the Bronze and Iron Ages, these regional maps will show the face of the land as it then was, with forests, marshes and coast-line (when necessary) restored; and the distribution of man and his works will be marked on them in coloured symbols. In another part of the same room will be photographs of living (or by then perhaps recently extinct) primitive peoples in a kindred state of culture, with a few of their implements and so forth in cases for comparison. Maps, for which there is no room or place in the scheme, will be framed and set in revolving stands, such as may be seen in picture-galleries; pictures will be similarly exhibited.

When we come at last to the point where many museums and almost all 'historical' text-books now begin — to the so-called historical period — the same general arrangement of time and space will be followed, but adaptations will be made to suit the nature of the material. There must not be any too rigid system of regions or periods, but each will be selected in accordance with the actual events that occurred. In the early days the Aegean, Egypt, Babylonia, India and China are obvious examples of regions, but we shall not forget to show fully what was happening in other countries when the civilisation of these regions was at its height. Statues and portraits of great men—Khufu, Merenptah, Akhnaten, Hammurabi, Asoka—will dominate the rooms of their respective periods. There is no reason why we should not admit imaginative portraits and other work of good modern artists — nay more, we may even hope that our galleries may inspire them. And when in our progress down the corridor of Time we come to the room where Greece is to be found, and see the flower of classical art gradually unfolding through the centuries and bursting into full blossom when at last the time was ripe—but here the wealth of material forbids discussion. Sufficient that even here we shall not lose sight of the time and space treatment, nor lose our sense of proportion. We need not fear that classic Greece will suffer harm at the hands of Science which was born upon her shores. Rather will she gain by an arrangement which brings out her unique position in the evolution of culture. Is it likely that she will lose by a comparison between her culture in the fifth century and that of, say, contemporary Egypt, Rome or Western Europe ? —a comparison that, in our museum, will force itself upon the attention.

Enough has been said to show how later ages will be portrayed. We shall not linger over the details of mediaeval turmoils, but when desirable shall show them succinctly by maps. The fact of conflict here is generally more important (as a warning) than its details. Briefly, the post-Roman galleries will show the lapse of culture during the Dark Ages, its gradual rise during the second millennium, the encroachment of man upon nature —in West and North Europe by the clearing of the forests and draining of marshes. The expansion of knowledge of the earth's surface will be shown, of course, by maps — the voyages not only of Europeans but also of Arabs and Chinese. For we are concerned not merely with the discoveries made by the human groups from which we ourselves derive, but with the discovery of the earth by man. Every continent will be as fully represented as knowledge permits.

When we come to the present day our method of treatment will be the same. The culture of each region will be shown in precisely similar fashion. Only I expect there will be some 'annexes' for environment. One will be devoted to meteorology. There will be large globes showing typical weather conditions at a given moment over the whole world—the distribution of high and low pressure-systems, the direction and force of the wind, the amount of cloud, rain and snow. Three dimensional glass-covered globes will show the currents of the upper air. In another room will be globes showing the vegetation of the earth, natural and artificial. Cases will contain an impartial assortment of typical (not selected) products of each region, such as may sometimes be seen in the windows of a colonial agency in London. Regions capable of agricultural development will be indicated. In another will be a geological map of the world on a globe, with typical specimens of important or common rocks and soils round the walls, and photographs of their outcrops. On another globe will be marked the principal communications of the world—railways, roads, canals, air-routes. On another will be shown nothing but the relief of the globe (unobscured by an umbrella of longitudes)—mountains and ocean-depths and snow-caps. On another will be the chief races of mankind and their distribution ; on another the chief mineral areas (if by then these have retained any practical importance).

The World Museum will not stop at the present. The rooms devoted to possibilities of the future will be amongst the most attractive of all. Any reasonable device for the improvement of life will find a place—schemes for using the tides, street and city plans (if there are cities—if not, city regions), ways of beautifying necessary objects, not by secondary and often hideous ' ornament ' (as now), but by closer adaptation of design to ends. Most of the exhibits will be models, and, like those in other rooms, they will be changed frequently.

At last at the end of the whole long corridor, in a room without transepts, there will be a single globe and nothing else. It is the moon, bare, cold and lifeless ; for what the moon is now the earth will be some day.

I rather fancy that on each side of the central corridor certain epoch-making innovations will be shown historically, each in its proper chronological place. Such are, for instance, the power of progression, the development of the senses, the upright posture, the power of flight, navigation (from the dug-out canoe to the U-boat), the discovery of fire, the invention of writing and speech, the development of tools and of the arts, the rise and fall of warfare, the invention of matches and machinery, the evolution of the idea of God. I hope also that the somewhat rigid system of time and space will not be carried too far in any one department. Within the limits of a room free play will be allowed for the exercise of the curator's imagination. So long as he keeps within bounds that will be all to the good. One does not want a row of stereotyped atrocities, differing only in the contents of the cases. One wants each room (or whatever the area of subdivision be) to reflect something of the intelligent care bestowed by its guardian, and to differ from its neighbour as one rose differs from another.

It pleases me to place the World Museum in America, the continent of big things. I like to think that some day the American tourist will cease rushing about Europe like a schoolboy, peeping at a few accidentally 'historical' sites and decaying ruins, and that he will turn instead to such a monument of all time in his own land. I like to think of it, further, as the goal of pilgrims from every part of the world, the Mecca of mankind; surrounded like an Italian shrine by great hostels, its cases enriched by offerings contributed in friendly rivalry by every country of the earth.

CHAPTER XIX

CONCLUSION

AND what, dear reader, is the use of archaeology? As well ask the artist the use of painting pictures, or the musician the use of an organ. All knowledge is one, whether ' useful ' or not : he alone can understand in whom lives the love of beauty or the love of knowledge. The archaeologist who tries to re-create the past is like a craftsman at work upon a great building. At first he sees but dimly the plan of the whole, but as he warms to his work it gradually unfolds itself before him. Now and then he pauses and steps back to survey his work at a distance. He sees it as an organic part of the growing building; he sees where it falls short and where it is fashioned aright; and he returns to his task with refreshed vigour.

So, too, the archaeologist watches his map or plan grow before his eyes. For days he may be buried deep in problems of detail that to another might seem to lead nowhere — tramping perhaps all day over stubborn clay-lands, or wrestling with impenetrable undergrowth. But all the time he knows that in the evening, when at ease before a cosy fire he reviews the day's work, one stone the more will swing into its place, perhaps a cornerstone. There is no hope of communicating to another the intense satisfaction that comes from watching thus the daily growing map. It is the delight of an artist in his work; and the secret lies in observing the unities of time and space. He may be engaged in constructing two buildings at once, but they must not be built upon the same plot of ground. Upon the map of, say, Roman Wessex, there must not appear, even in meditation, earlier monuments (such as barrows) which, though existing then, had no more place in Roman life than in the life of to-day; nor later monuments which had not yet been erected. The growing map is the source of all inspiration; to work without it as a goal is to wander aimlessly into blind alleys.[1] Without a plan the excavation of a site is valueless.

It is this feeling of contributing to a larger scheme that cheers him in the midst of labours often dull and trivial. Without it such work would be intolerable. He knows that such progress, if slow, is doubly sure, and that only honest work counts; and he knows, too, that his own clear-cut ashlar in the temple of knowledge will fit into a scheme

[1] I do not wish to seem to underrate such non-geographical work as the evolution of types, which belongs to the time-aspect and is of the highest value. But work of this kind too will eventually find its way on to a map, though at the outset the map lies in the background.

which he cannot fully comprehend. But if he is in space a plodder, he travels through time upon the magic carpet of imagination. He sees the nations rise and fall before him like puppets in a show. ' The man who knows and dwells in history adds a new dimension to his existence; he no longer lives in the one plane of present ways and thoughts, he lives in the whole space of life, past, present and dimly future.' For his gaze is not directed backwards from the present; rather it ranges ever forwards from the past into the future. Like the traveller who has reached at evening the summit of a lofty pass, he scans with eager eyes the new landscape opening out before him; ever hoping amongst the low-lying valley mists to catch one glimpse of the Town of Heart's Delight.

> Take not that vision from my ken—
> Oh, whatsoe'er may spoil or speed.
> Help me to need no aid from men
> That I may help such men as need!

THE END

BIBLIOLIFE

Old Books Deserve a New Life
www.bibliolife.com

Did you know that you can get most of our titles in our trademark **EasyScript**™ print format? **EasyScript**™ provides readers with a larger than average typeface, for a reading experience that's easier on the eyes.

Did you know that we have an ever-growing collection of books in many languages?

Order online:
www.bibliolife.com/store

Or to exclusively browse our **EasyScript**™ collection:
www.bibliogrande.com

At BiblioLife, we aim to make knowledge more accessible by making thousands of titles available to you – quickly and affordably.

Contact us:
BiblioLife
PO Box 21206
Charleston, SC 29413